THE VOICES OF GENESIS

The
VOICES
of
GENESIS

LISTENING TO THE SPIRITS
ON THE ECSTATIC JOURNEY
TO ENLIGHTENMENT IN THE GARDEN

NICHOLAS E. BRINK, PH.D.

Red Elixir
Rhinebeck, New York

Paperback ISBN 978-1-960090-64-5
eBook ISBN 978-1-960090-65-2

Library of Congress Control Number 2024907463

Book design by Colin Rolfe

Red Elixir is an imprint of Monkfish Book Publishing Company

Red Elixir
22 East Market Street, Suite 304
Rhinebeck, New York 12572
(845) 876-4861
monkfishpublishing.com

Contents

RAYMOND HILLIS, PH.D.

Foreword

Of all the dichotomies in human experience, one of the most prevalent is that between the "known" and the "unknown." In one of the more famous quotes from contemporary political discourse, then Secretary of Defense in the United States Donald Rumsfeld, responding to a reporter asking for more definitive answers about the status of a military action, replied "There are known knowns, things we know we know; and there are known unknowns, things that we know we don't know. But there are also unknown unknowns, things we do not know we don't know." This was initially received by the public as an attempt to be humorous, or cute. Some saw it as just plain silly. And it became for a time a "go to" reply when one was asked what the truth about something was. And yet the statement was indeed a quite accurate reflection of what we humans rather desperately want to be true about our daily world. We want to be able to trust what it deemed "known" to stay that way; and then we are reluctantly willing to allow what lies beneath some of what we experience is, but only for the moment, deemed "unknown." One reasonable definition of progress itself, in fact, can be seen in the ability to move, over time, aspects of our experience from the unknown column to the known.

In this way, it must have felt like great progress when, in the 4th century B.C., Greek philosophers replaced the then accepted "knowledge" that the earth was a flat point in a flat universe with the new idea that the earth was, in fact, spherical, and was at the center of a spherical universe. Something unknown was believed to have become known. The unknown realm had become just a bit smaller, the boundary between that and the known realm had been moved just a bit and enlarged what we knew. Or so we thought at the time. And this understanding was securely held in the "known" category for around two millennia until it was proposed that this was not, indeed, true. At that point, something from the known category crossed back into the unknown, which Copernicus dealt with by proposing a new model in which the earth orbited around the sun, which was the true center of a single universe.

This shift brought a violent response initially from those who had built a substantial reality around the geocentric model. Some individuals were burned at the stake for promoting it because it undermined powerful religious structures that had formed around that no longer "known" model. And yet, out of the new heliocentric model came a profound change in our understanding of the nature of the entire universe, a new model that took up residence in the realm of the known. And yet, inevitably that model too moved back into the realm of the unknown when we learned that even the sun is not the center of our universe. It was replaced with a model of a vast, single universe the center of which is simply not known.

And now, once again, the known model has been shifted back into the unknown as astronomers with ever stronger telescopes propose the existence, in as yet totally unknown form, of multiple universes, possibly countless parallel realities, and so on.

This is a noetic dance of cosmic proportions, in which one can begin to imagine that the size of the "ultimately" known world, that which is secure in the "known knowns" column, is much smaller than was previously thought. And increasingly we are confronted with the need to "deconstruct" our conceptual understandings to make room for reconstruction of new models which will seem known for a time, only to require of themselves subsequent rounds of deconstruction as new experience require.

Stephan Gould gave, some 35 years ago, new substance to this phenomenon in his book "Time's Arrow, Time's Cycle: Myth and Metaphor in the Discovery of Geological Time" (1987). He proposed that our notion of progress as a linear increasing of the realm of what is known is deceptive, because time itself is not linear, but circular in nature. In such a world, "progress" involves moving around a repeating circle of construction and deconstruction of conceptual realities, a rhythmic dance back and forth between the realms of the unknown and the known. In such a model, there can be just as much "progress" in unknowing something that has outgrown its time as there is in knowing something new. This kind of progress is not a continuous addition of layers of understanding upon what is already known, but a true deconstructing of the old so that the new may be born. It requires a continuous ability to relinquish what we thought we knew to make room for the new knowledge, a never-ending cycle of death and rebirth, as it were, in the realm of knowledge, and, therefore, in the realm of truth itself as we know it. And this takes place on the levels of personal life, cultural constructs, and assumptions about humanity as a whole.

Two concepts arise here: they are those of mystery and history. On the one hand, we have the unknown, the realm of mystery; on the other hand, is the realm of history, the accumulation of what is known, at least for the moment. In this way, we like to think that mystery offers the opportunity to uncloak what it is holding, and certainly this is a primary objective of, among other things, the scientific method. This is also our usual definition of progress itself. In this form, progress becomes a linear expansion of what is considered known alongside a linear contraction of the unknown. Or, in other words, progress involves turning mystery into history. But this formulation leaves out half of the story, for it is equally valuable "progress" to turn history back into mystery when the old "known" no longer functions. In other words, progress itself is a circular function: mystery into history, and back into mystery again as experience evolves.

The title of Gould's book gives us a link to bring this discussion to bear upon the present book by Nicholas Brink, because both give a central role to "myth." The concept of myth carries vastly different value depending upon its use. We can say "That's just a myth", intending to utterly invalidate a point of view. In such a usage we set myth and truth as opposites. But we can also give vast support to something by saying, "That is of mythic proportions." This usage does not claim truth or untruth for something, but expresses an importance of exploring it further. This latter understanding is closer to the actual meaning of the word. And as such it implies the need to explore the mythic element further to see whatever additional truths, it might reveal. In this sense, we view myths and the stories they contain as preserving essential truths held by prior civilizations. To those ancient peoples, these stories were not at all mythical. They were considered factual. They were history itself.

Because we have not lived in the same experiential world they encountered, we have lost the "living" quality of the accounts of events that they narrate in their myths, events they took to be in the known world; events that were part of their history and recorded for handing down to future peoples, not because they made good stories, but because they were true.

As we have discovered these ancient myths, we have tended to treat them as fictional tales, not particularly different from what we call "fairytales" today. But there is a vital, essential difference between the two. The classical myths were not written as fiction, they were accounts of what the people who recorded them experienced and believed to be true, and they contained an imperative that their truths be passed forward. Fairytales, on the other hand, were and still are written to entertain and educate, often intended to teach young readers, in an enjoyable format, some truths about life that they will likely need as they mature. They make no claim whatever to being historical.

Throughout the twentieth century a movement arose, particularly among the psychoanalytic community, to unearth the enduring meaning, or truths, contained beneath the story-level details in ancient mythology. Freud and Jung, among others, led this movement, and their intellectual descendants continue to this day to illuminate the "meanings" for today's individuals and cultures that each myth carries forward, even as the events described are no longer held to have actually occurred. This field of study has arisen within the general field of psychology because, as Victor Frankl

(Man's Search for Meaning, 1945) proposed, it is in finding a sense of the "meaning" of one's life that one obtains a "why" for living and gives the motive to discover the more practical "hows" for living.

Seen in this way, ancient myths become treasure troves for finding the whys for one's own life. The "hows" they include tend to be applicable mostly to the times in which they were written. If we get caught up in those details, we are likely to dismiss the myth itself as too dated to be of relevance today. But if we focus upon the "meaning" of the story, often amplified by symbolism that has come to be seen as carrying such meaning in a timeless manner, we can find personal and cultural value that is as true today as when the story originated.

The present book is focused upon that task.

This volume is the tenth this author has produced dealing with mythology and personal growth. He began, long ago now, with a detailed explication of Norse mythology, due in part to his own family history. He has subsequently made his way through a large number of myths from a variety of cultures. The present volume takes on seven mythic stories contained in the biblical book of Genesis. As with prior volumes, his methods for revealing the underlying meanings of these myths include a significant focus upon the techniques contained in the practice of Ecstatic Trance as taught by the Cuyamungue Institute (founded by Felicitas D. Goodman) and located near Santa Fe, New Mexico.

The core of this text focuses, in depth, on reports of five practitioners who came together to enter seven sessions of ecstatic trance focusing upon one myth at a time. In the first part of this section of the book, the focus is upon the "collective" meanings that are revealed to each participant and the group as a whole. This section presents levels of meaning that transcend each individual's personal life. Then there is a final section in which each individual reports the intensely personal meanings each myth was found to carry about their own separate life. This material gives the reader a chance to see not only the collective meanings carried in common for all of us but also a view of how the same story can yield quite individualized meaning for each of us depending upon our own life circumstances. Each reader can also take a personal journey into the depths of the psychological world these myths explore.

The material on these pages reveals a world of imagination, symbolism, and dream imagery that lives within each of us, and gives us a strong set of tools for exploring the "unknown" world around - and especially within - each of us, and a way of moving some of that world of mystery into the realm of being "known", becoming part of our personal history.

You are standing at the point of the ever-shifting intersection between the worlds of the known and the unknown within you. There is much to be discovered.

Raymond Hillis, Professor Emeritus, Counseling, California State University, Los Angeles, now living in Santa Fe, New Mexico

Preface

In my youth, I attended a Presbyterian Church where I learned there are five aspects of prayer: glorification, thanksgiving, forgiveness, intersession, and petition. Then in college, I realized that listening was missing. I was taught that God listened, but how were we to listen? Looking back now, I see how listening beyond my five senses became a life quest. In psychology, I took a deep interest in dreams and how to interpret them. In my practice of psychology, dream-work and hypnosis became central to my work. Upon graduation, we moved to Pennsylvania where we attended the nearby Quaker Meeting and worshiped in silent meditation. Then, most recently I have become a certified instructor of ecstatic or shamanic trance. All these modes of listening from beyond my five senses have been central in my life.

Listening to the spirits of the Earth Goddess gave the early hunter-gatherers direction in life. The seven stories of Genesis, initially passed down by the scalds or storytellers of the time, were listened to as dreams were listened to, before being recorded in the Torah and Old Testament. For Joseph of the coat of many colors, listening through dreams led him to become the governor of Egypt.

In our journey of listening to the spirits of Genesis using ecstatic trance, the group of five of us found deeper dimensions to these seven stories. First, the biblical serpent, the source of wisdom in the hunter and gatherer world of matriarchy, became a snake of the devil. The dichotomy of good vs. evil as taught by the serpent creates the separation experienced in the world of patriarchy, used as an avenue to gain power and control. We have lived in this world of separation for several millennia, but listening to the spirits led the five of us to overcome this patriarchal power and control by returning us to the compassionate world of matriarchy. Now, we can value with compassion the great diversity in which we live, diversity that was a source of the experiences of patriarchal separation.

Second, as we proceed through the stories of Genesis, we see the Chosen People and the Promised Land of Israel as reflections of patriarchal separation. We as a group were led to recognize the Promised Land as the return to the Garden of the Matriarchal World of the Creatrix. She is everywhere, wherever we may be, and we are all the Goddess's Chosen People. The Promised Land for Joseph was in Egypt where he became governor. The Goddess does not create patriarchal separation, but she is the gateway in our return to the ever-present Garden of Eden.

A third trance experience showed the group that listening to one's emotions brings resolution to the separation of good vs. evil. These experiences thus uncovered deeper meanings of the Stories of Genesis.

The book continues to examine what each of the five of us learned personally in this journey to enlightenment. What we learned provided us with personal growth to prepare us for entering the new world of the Garden. During the last several millennia of living in the patriarchal world, reality has been limited to that which comes to us through our five senses of sight, sound, smell, taste, and touch. We listened to these stories of Genesis in this limited way as literal history. Now, in listening to the spirits, we come to them in a state of enlightenment.

Introduction

For the last 2500 years, we have lived in an era of rational consciousness in which we have believed that reality comes only through the
five senses of sight, sound, smell, taste, and touch. We have rejected
or considered as superstitious and unreal that which comes from
beyond these senses, such as from dreams. Yet dreams were important in the stories of the Bible such as the dreams interpreted by
Joseph, interpretations that led him to become Governor of Egypt.

For the last century, dreams and other altered states of consciousness have come back into prominence as seen in their effective use in psychotherapy, and psychoanalysis, and in the number
of people who are part of such organizations as The International
Association for the Study of Dreams, and the American Society of
Clinical Hypnosis. As a clinical psychologist, I learned early of the
importance of dreams in the process of psychotherapy. My interest
in working with dreams brought alive within me a deepening interest in the metaphoric language of dreams and the myths that arose
from the dreams of our distant hunting and gathering ancestors.
One myth that I found most powerful in my work as a psychologist,
recorded about a thousand years ago by Snorri Sturluson[1] in his
book *The Prose Edda,* is the story of the Norse Pantheon of Deities,
including Odin and Thor. This myth describes overcoming the torment caused by the trickster god Loki and his three monster children, Jormungand, Hel, and Fenrir. It beautifully lays out a map of
the course of psychotherapy for overcoming the tormentors in life.
The experience of reading this myth brought alive within me the
deeper meaning of many other myths such as *The Twelve Labors of
Hercules*[2] for overcoming twelve of his tormentors, returning him to

his rightful role as the son of the supreme god Zeus. Another myth is the Old English story of *Beowulf* [3] who overcame two tormenting monsters, Grendel and Grendel's mother, to become the king of the Geats as I describe in my book, *Grendel and His Mother: Healing the Traumas of Childhood Through Dreams, Imagery and Hypnosis.*

Of special interest and curiosity in the *Prose Edda* is the story of Idunn and her garden. In the Garden of Idunn she grows the golden apples that keep young the gods of the ancient north, including Odin, the god of gods, and the warrior god Thor, the most powerful though impulsive deity. Thor's human quality of impulsiveness repeatedly gets him in trouble.

This story of the Garden of Idunn rekindled my interest in finding the deeper meaning of the Garden of Eden, and the stories of the Biblical Book of Genesis brewed in the back of my mind for several years. When I read Matthew Wood's book, *Seven Herbs: Plants as Teachers* [4], these thoughts moved to the forefront. Matthew Wood is an herbalist who values the spiritual energy of seven herbs that carried him into a deeper understanding of the seven stories of the book of Genesis, the stories of Adam and Eve, Cain and Abel, Noah and the Ark, Abraham, Isaac, Jacob, and Joseph. Upon reading his book and in personal communication with him, Matthew, a longtime birthright Quaker, asked me to preview his more recent manuscript, *Seven Guideposts on the Spiritual Path: The Shamanic Stories of Genesis,* [5] that describes his own journey through these seven stories. With my background as a convinced Quaker, I found his journey through these stories deeply inspiring.

The metaphoric language of myths is often quite mysterious, and it may be difficult to understand how they personally apply to the reader. The researchers of dreams offer many techniques for interpreting dreams. One of the simplest, which I learned first, is the Gestalt technique of taking each segment of a dream and ask, "What part of me does the segment describe?" [6] For example, if in a dream I spill paint on the floor, I might ask, "What part of me is making a mess?" Then bringing together the meaning of each segment provides a deeper personal understanding of the dream.

But dreams likely have many layers of meaning, so holding onto the dream over time can open more and more doors to its personal meaning.

My book, *Loki's Children: A Healing Story of Antiquity, Shamanism and Psychotherapy,*[7] takes the reader on a journey to such deeper understanding. But what is the connection between the Norse Goddess Idunn and the Biblical Eden? The stories of the Book of Genesis, originally passed down orally by the bards of the tribes of a preliterate society, are stories that can be considered mythical. Listening to them as myths brings to them a new and deeper understanding of their meaning. This book brings us to a deeper personal understanding of these stories that many Judeo-Christians have thought of as historic or literal truths as they have listened to them during the era of rational consciousness, an era that denies the deeper important meaning of that which is mythical. One book of an early version of the Bible, *The Book of Enoch,* was deleted from the Bible in 364 A.D. because it was considered mythical.

The five of us in our ecstatic trance group journeyed through the seven stories of Genesis to explore their deeper meaning, a journey that calls upon the altered state of consciousness of ecstatic or shamanic trance as described in Chapter 2, a state of consciousness available to our preliterate ancestors. We found in our metaphoric journeys as a group commonality that brought the five of us to a deeper and relatively consistent understanding of the story's deeper meaning as described in Part II of the book, as well as of personal growth for each person in the group.

Part I

Setting *the* Stage

CHAPTER 1

To Begin

The stories of Genesis: of Adam and Eve, Cain and Abel, Noah and the Ark, Abraham, Isaac, Jacob, and Joseph, have been told and retold for many generations, but those who believe they are literal or factual history overlook the deeper meaning found in them. Like the myths of antiquity, of the Earth's ancient cultures, they have many deeper layers of meaning that are sorely missed when read as literal and historical truth. These archetypal narratives were passed down orally by storytellers skilled at memorizing lengthy stories before they were first recorded about 6000 years ago. When listening to them from beyond our limited five senses of sight, sound, smell, taste, and touch, these stories reveal deeper layers of meaning. Listening from beyond our five senses to these stories open many more dimensions, just as we would listen to our nighttime dreams[1], the experiences in our imagination[2], other trance experiences from altered-states-of-consciousness such as hypnotic and ecstatic trance[3], and what I call morning revere[4], the consciousness state of just waking from sleep and letting the mind flow to see where it takes you.

As a child growing up in a churchgoing family, I heard some of these stories in Sunday School and in youth bible studies, primarily the stories of Adam and Eve, Noah and the Ark, and Joseph with his coat of many colors. How did I come to be so interested in the art of listening to that which lies beyond my five senses? Having learned as a Presbyterian that there are five elements to prayer: glorification, thanksgiving, forgiveness, petition, and intercession, I eventually realized that what was missing was listening. This change in my understanding of prayer opened a few new doors in my life. In college at UCLA, while majoring in psychology, I took an interest in the power of dreams, dreams that come from beyond the five senses. In my practice as a psychologist, the use of hypnosis and guided imagery became central, altered states of consciousness that took me beyond the five senses. In moving to Pennsylvania, I left the church of my youth and began attending a Quaker Meeting where the meeting is held in silent meditation of listening to the spirits, spirits that would move me and others to speak. Professionally, I became the president of the American Association for the Study of Mental Imagery and a member of the Board of Directors of the International Association for the Study of Dreams.

At that time, I became increasingly deaf such that I had to leave my professional life as a clinical psychologist. Though I eventually had surgery in 2017 to receive a cochlear implant, which has helped considerably in my ability to listen with my ears, I found myself in the world of listening to the spirits from beyond my rational mind. In 2004, I went a step further in the pursuit of listening to the beyond. I discovered the power of ecstatic trance, trance induced by rapid stimulation to the nervous system by drumming or rattling as researched by the anthropologist Felicitas Goodman. Now I have in my spiritual repertoire the skill of listening to the spirits through dreams, hypnotic trance, meditation, waking revere, and ecstatic or shamanic trance. I became a certified instructor of ecstatic trance in 2011 and continue to practice and teach this shamanic form of trance, not unlike the trance experiences of our hunting and gathering ancestors. With ecstatic trance, I use my ears considerably less.

Then in 2012, I became the Director of Research for Felicitas Goodman's Cuyamungue Institute and in this capacity, I have sought to answer the question of where ecstatic trance can take a person, the content of seven of my published books.

Mythical Aspects of The Seven Stories

Typical of the myths of antiquity, the ancient gods and goddesses exhibit the qualities and emotions of humans. To name a few of these human emotions, the Greek and Roman myths portray the deities as being jealous, angry, impulsive, and vulnerable to the torment of various monsters as seen in the twelve labors of Hercules. In Nordic Mythology of which I am most familiar, Thor is quick to lose his temper, and Loki continually confronts the gods of their hypocrisies. The gods respond to Loki with anger and finally restrain him until the final battle, Ragnarök, when he breaks free of his bonds to fight. The high and all-knowing god, Odin, fears Fenrir, the ever-growing wolf, knowing that his own death will come in the jaws of Fenrir. All these feelings are typical of humans, but not what one might expect from an all-powerful creator god. Even the Christian God holds these emotions when described as a jealous god, and a god of wrath as seen in his punishment of those he created by throwing them out of the Garden of Eden, cursing Cain to wander an unproductive earth, and destroying in the flood all those whose behavior diverged from what pleased Him. Again, these are human qualities not expected in an all-powerful and loving God or Goddess.

The Language of Mythology

The redeeming quality of these mythic stories of antiquity, including the stories of Genesis, is what they have embedded spiritually within them, spiritual experiences of healing, personal growth, and how to live sustainably upon our one and only Earth. These spiritual stories are told in a poetic language, the language of metaphor. We are all familiar with this poetic or metaphoric language, the language of song, because it is the language of our nighttime dreams. Though many may discount the deeper meaning of their dreams, opening oneself to these deeper meanings opens the door to healing and personal growth. Many who read the Bible discount their dreams, yet the dreams in the Bible play a prominent role, especially in the story of Joseph, the Joseph with his coat of many colors, found in the Book of Genesis.

The understanding of these metaphoric stories may not be

immediate since they are told in this secret language with hidden meaning, but each character and element of the story, when
thought of as a personal spirit guide, opens the door to understanding them as coming from the world of the spirits. One way to understand their deeper meaning as described in the Introduction is to
ask, "What part of me does each character or element of the dream
represent?"

The Voice of the Lord

In these stories, Adam and Eve, Cain and Abel, and Noah hear the
voice of the Lord as coming from beyond our five senses, but after
the Tower of Babel, Abraham, Isaac, Jacob, and Joseph experience
the voice of the Lord indirectly in dreams and visions. Julian Jaynes[5]
explains this change in human consciousness as evolutionary, a
neurological change in the brain where that which arises in the
right hemisphere no longer seems to come from outside the person. The two hemispheres have become integrated and what arises
in the right hemisphere is heard as coming from within. The slow
process of evolutionary change suggests that the three initial stories
are much more ancient than the time when they were recorded in
the Torah.

Because the people of the time were no longer hearing the voice
of God coming from the beyond, they built a tower, the Tower of
Babel, in their attempt to get closer to God to hear his voice again.
But with this evolutionary neurological change, people began hearing the voice when in an altered state of consciousness such as in
dreams, hypnosis, and ecstatic trance visions.

Since the Tower the voices heard are much broader, voices that
speak in the language of metaphor, voices of the spirits of the Earth
that tell us what we need for our health, for personal growth, and
how to live sustainably without destroying the Earth. These voices
are of the many spirits of our creator, our Great Earth Mother. This
current evolutionary change in consciousness Jean Gebser[6] refers to
as time-free transparency, of that which is experienced free of time

and transparent or visible in our dreams and other trance experiences. This change takes us back to our *Ever-Present Origin*, the title of Gebser's book, to the way our hunter-gatherer ancestors experienced life in their ability to commune with the spirits of their ancestors and of the Earth, the world of the spirits.

Metaphoric Themes that bring us back to the Garden

The metaphoric and mythical stories of Genesis come from the world of the spirits, and when listened to and examined metaphorically, their much deeper meaning becomes clear beyond the simply literal history of how many or most people read them. "The people who wrote the book of Genesis were seers who fathomed the mysteries of human nature and then rendered their findings into stories which any child would be able to understand[7]. If read with a spiritual eye, with sensitivity to their poetic meaning, metaphor, and their relevance to spiritual existence, Genesis proves to be a detailed and thorough guide to the development of a spiritual life[8]."

The themes for the journey back to the Garden revolve around death and rebirth, as seen in the far-reaching parallels in many other cultures of overcoming the obstacles to the Garden. These obstacles, created by a patriarchal God who plays favorites with the dichotomies of good and evil, when overcome with the dissolution of this dichotomous separation, the Gate to the Garden, to the Promised Land, is again opened.

Death and Rebirth

Another reason we consider these seven stories of Genesis metaphoric, to be interpreted for their deeper meaning, is the fact that we find similar or parallel archetypal stories in many other cultures, e.g., the ancient Nordic story of the Garden of Idunn[9] and her golden apples that keep the gods young. When a giant kidnaps Idunn, the gods aged rapidly towards death, but through Loki's tricks, Idunn returns, and the gods are reborn in youthful strength. In the Egyptian story of Osiris[10], his jealous brother cuts him into pieces after which his wife or sister, Isis, collects all the pieces and wraps them together to bring him back to life. We find a similar death and rebirth experience in the Finnish Kalevala story with the death and dismemberment of the Shepherd of the North, Lemminkainen, because of his disrespectful behavior. He falls into the river of death, but his mother knows of his death when she sees blood flowing from his hairbrush, thus she sets out to find him. When she finds his pieces in the river, she puts him back together, and a bee sting brings him back to life. These stories are reminiscent of the story of the death of Abel at the hands of his brother Cain. The Lord hearing cries from Abel's blood soaking the Earth is his rebirth, the rebirth of his voice. The Lord thus curses Cain: "When you till the ground, it shall not henceforth yield her strength to you, and you shall be a fugitive from the Earth."

These death-rebirth experiences show us the way back to the Garden of Eden, a rebirth in Paradise, the Promised Land, a rebirth that is happening in this new era or time-free transparency.

Far-Reaching Parallels to the Stories of Genesis

David Elkington, in his book, *The Ancient Language of Sacred Sound*[12], finds that there are many linguistic cognates to the names Jesus, Christ, Mary and Anne the mother of Mary, that exist among the deities of Egypt, Greece, the Celts, Norse, and around the world, even in Central and South America. The incredible parallels and similarities between Christian beliefs and those of these more ancient religions show that the stories of Jesus and Christianity are older than the 3500-year-old Torah, or the 2000-year-old biblical stories of the birth and the life of Jesus. For example, in one pre-Islamic Arabic story, Issa, whose name is related linguistically to Jesus, was born of Maryam, crucified, and rose again from the dead on the third day.

Our Western culture has only one superhero, Jesus, while the East has many. In these other stories, the hero, being both mortal and divine, dies a terrible death and journeys to hell before rising to immortality in paradise. He is most often the son of a goddess and a not-so-divine father, though in Western mythologies he is a son of God and born of a virgin mother. As the divine hero grows from childhood to adulthood, he becomes the miracle maker, the savior "god-man," a healer and seer, e.g., feeding the five thousand and turning water to wine. He rises after his death to become divine.

The linguistic analysis of the names of the hero reveals connections to many cultures, e.g., the Greek God Hercules, the Egyptian Horus, and the Genesis story of Abram whose name gains an "H" when changed to Abraham. The name Jesus linguistically connects to the Egyptian Gisa, Gaia, and the names Kaiser, Caesar, and Czar, all deifying titles. Similarly, Osiris is the Greek version of the Egyptian Asir, and with my research into the ancient Nordic deities, I would add Aesir, the tribal name of the Nordic deities.

Such words and their cognates, as found in many languages and cultures, show the power of these archetypal words/concepts. From Psalms 33.6, the word of the Lord made the heavens and, by the breath of his mouth, all their hosts. Also, the Egyptian hieroglyph for the divine word of the creator is the serpent. According to Laird Scranton[13], the serpent is the bringer of knowledge for so many of the earlier world religions, knowledge that takes humanity out of the innocence of their new creation into the broader world of knowledge, bringing them into the world of separation with it many dichotomies.

According to Ashra Kwesi[14], the origin of the Adam and Eve story came much earlier in African-Egyptian mythology, as seen in the story depicted in the Rameseum in Kemet, Egypt. We all came from the divine principle of the sacred womb, the matriarchal Goddess Principle that gave us divine wisdom and life from the tree of divine wisdom and divine life. This newly uncovered meaning of the story of Adam and Eve is not of the patriarchal tree of good and evil, the opposites or dichotomies that come to us through the serpent of the devil. For a divine king to rule from his throne, he needs the wisdom from the tree of divine life and wisdom gained from the divine principle of the sacred womb. Eating of the fruit of the tree of divine wisdom and life brings one wisdom and life and not the dichotomy of opposites of good vs. evil, the patriarchal separation we have suffered for several thousand years.

Overcoming Obstacles to Regain Paradise

The journey of Greek Hercules[15] and his battles with his twelve tormentors is a journey towards regaining his rightful position among the gods as the son of Zeus and finding his way back to paradise. Similarly, Beowulf's[16] journey to become a King of the Geats requires that he kill the two tormentors of King Hrothgar, Grendel and Grendel's Mother, again a journey taking him to his rightful place in Paradise. Hel, Jormungand and Fenrir, the tormentors of Odin, the high god of the Norse, similarly die with the rebirth of the innocent Baldr in the final battle at Ragnarök. Though the number of stages required for these rebirths vary, each story shows the return journey to Paradise, as do the seven stories of Genesis. Matthew Wood finds the number seven an important number in many cultures, specifically regarding this return to the Garden, to be discussed in Chapter 3.

These stories show us that to journey back to the Garden we need to first resolve the personal problems that hinder us in this journey as I have written about in two books: *Grendel and His Mother*, and *Loki's Children*, personal journeys that open the gate to the Garden, the Promised Land.

Playing Favorites

The gods of these ancient stories frequently played favorites, creating painful and destructive dualities, e.g., by blessing one child but not his brother, or by choosing one tribe of people over another. Again, playing favorites is not a characteristic of a loving creator but a dysfunctional characteristic within the family or a problem in bringing people together from different tribal groups. For example, the creator god Odin favors the tribe of the gods and goddesses of the Aesir over those of the Vanir, a problem that creates an unwinnable war. The literal belief that God favored Abraham by giving him the land of Israel continues to instigate the conflict between the Israelis and the Palestinians, but as we shall see, as we move into the new age of time-free transparency, such dualities will dissolve with new respect and cooperation among people of great diversity.

With this rebirth in the Garden, we will find a rebirth of innocence and unity where our dualistic way of thinking created separation, a transformative rebirth of greater unity than ever experienced before. As stated by the Swedish writer and Mayanist, Carl Calleman:[17] "The separation from the divine source that the dualist frame of consciousness has caused will disappear as a result of the evolution of consciousness, and it has been said that this separation is the sole cause of human suffering."

These human characteristics and traits of a god are most typical of the stories of mythology, stories that have something important to impart, stories for healing, personal growth and of how to live sustainably on our one and only earth. The seven stories of the Biblical Book of Genesis are like these mythological stories initially passed down by the bards, scalds, shamans, and teachers of antiquity before being recorded around 6000 years ago.

The World of the Spirits

In the Christian belief of the Father, Son, and Holy Ghost, the Trinity, the Holy Ghost is the spirit of the Lord, the Holy Spirit that comes from beyond one's five senses of sight, sound, smell, taste, and touch. The Tower of Babel was a turning point in hearing the words of the Lord. Before the Tower, Adam and Eve, Cain and Abel, and Noah heard the words of the Lord directly as coming from an invisible god outside themselves, but after the Tower, the words of God came from within, indirectly through dreams and visions, through the spirits from beyond the five senses.

Dreams play a prominent role in the Bible, and the interpreters of dreams such as Joseph with the cloak of many colors brought him prominence in the eyes of the Egyptian Pharaoh. His interpretations relied upon each element or character of a dream, the dream spirits that come from beyond our five senses. These dream spirits speak in a hidden or metaphoric language, and to understand them, an interpreter of this metaphoric language such as Joseph is needed.

Looking back to our hunter-gatherer ancestors, Jean Gebser[18] believed that during the earliest era of consciousness, people lived in a dream-like state of hearing the spirits of the Earth as coming from the world of the spirits. Such writers as Rupert Sheldrake[19] and Ervin Laszlo[20] believe this world of the spirits comes from beyond our individual physiological brain from the universal consciousness, and is a reality, a world accessible through dreams and altered states of consciousness such as hypnotic and ecstatic trance. Carlos Castaneda[21] describes these two altered states of dreams and trance as dreaming and stalking. The dreamer enters the world of the spirits by letting go of thought, while the stalker is distracted from thought through drumming or rattling to seek answers with intent. Listening to the spirits was natural before the Tower of Babel as listened to by our hunter-gathering ancestors. Now, with our new understanding of consciousness, we are again hearing these spirits in Jean Gebser's new era of time-free transparency, an era which is becoming increasingly apparent.

The Seven Stories of Genesis

The sevenfold path or perception of life offered in the stories of Genesis takes us on a journey of leaving the Garden of Eden and the return to the Garden, the Promised Land. In the Garden, the innocence of the new creation or birth of Adam and Eve was a life of peace that lacked the separation of good and evil. When they gained the wisdom of the differences between good and evil, they lost this life of innocence. Their progeny, Cain and Abel, then lived in this new world of "wisdom," a new world of separation, strong with feelings that brought to Cain the feelings of jealousy such that he took the life of his brother. Then, as the generations passed, the corruption of the people increased and reached a crisis point that brought the great flood as called forth by the patriarchal God to destroy the corrupt and bring about a new birth at the time of Noah, Noah who had the faith to follow the words he heard from the Lord.

But then, through evolution, the people lost the ability to hear these words. Abraham, though, heard the words in his dreams and visions and faithfully followed them, finding in them the power to become rich with his flocks, vineyard, and the leader of the land of his people. For Isaac, the son of Abraham and Sarah, the dreams, and visions as experienced by his father, experiences of the Lord's promise, became an experiential reality when he discovered he too had the power of his father as the leader of his people of the Promised Land, thus he followed in his father's footsteps. But Jacob, the son of Isaac and Rebekah, struggled to prove to himself the reality of his dreams and visions. He fought against them like when he fought the Angel of the Lord in a dream, a fight that he won, thus proving to himself the reality of his visions from the world beyond his five senses. With this evolution in believing and finding strength in the experiences from beyond, from the world of the spirits, Joseph, Jacob and Rachel's son, listened to them and understood them such that he became prominent in the eyes of the Egyptian Pharaoh as an interpreter of dreams, showing that he had gained the ability to listen to that which was initially experienced in the innocence of Adam and Eve in the Garden of Eden.

This understanding of the evolution through the seven stories of Genesis is parallel to the same sevenfold view of the world held by the shamans of the many indigenous cultures as described by Matthew Wood.[22] After expulsion from the Garden and living within the new world of dichotomies that created the corruption the Lord destroyed in the flood, Abraham followed his dreams and visions when he accepted the words of the Lord to sacrificing his son. He thus gained the land given to him and his descendants. Isaac, the son of Abraham and Sarah, had to overcome his traumatic reaction to when his father held a knife over his head for him to experience the fact that the land given to Abraham was his. And Jacob, the son of Isaac and Rebekah, attained his spiritual self at the river crossing when he overcame his struggle with the angel of the Lord, validating that the land given to his grandfather and his grandfather's descendants was his too. Joseph was comfortable with this belief and of being blessed with the ability to interpret dreams that brought him prominence in the land of Egypt. His spirituality no longer depended on the land that is now Israel, but on the land upon which he dwelt, the Promised Land.

CHAPTER 2

Ecstatic Trance

In journeying through the seven stories of Genesis to find their deeper meaning, the five of us used ecstatic trance as researched by the anthropologist Felicitas Goodman.[1] Goodman, a Hungarian linguist educated in Germany was fluent in about 20 languages. In pursuing her Doctorate at Ohio State University, she recognized that the speaking in tongues in the apostolic churches was a form of ecstatic trance, thus she went to Mexico and observed the speaking in tongues in both Mayan speaking and Spanish speaking apostolic churches. She concluded that there were four elements in the church experience that brought members of the congregations to speak in tongues:

- A special or sacred space such as the church.
- An expectation and belief that speaking in tongues is special, a divine language unknown to the speaker.
- A period to quiet one's mind as in prayer.
- Rapid stimulation to the nervous system as with hand clapping, drumming, or rattling.

She then returned to Denison University where she was teaching and created a more indigenous ritual incorporating these four elements:

- Discussing with the students what to expect in trance.
- Creating a sacred space with smudging and calling the spirits from each direction.
- Quieting the mind with five minutes of silence while following one's breath.
- Inducing trance with the beat of a rattle or drum at approximately 210 beats per minute for 15 minutes.

She found the students went into a decent trance, but the trance experience was undirected. In the church, the belief and expectation of speaking in tongues gave the congregants direction. Sometime later Goodman read an article by V. F. Emerson,[2] a Canadian psychologist who was researching the effects of various meditation postures on the body, measuring such factors as breathing rate, bowel motility, skin moisture and heart rate. He found different postures had different effects on the body. This led Goodman to examine pictures and ancient figurines from the hunter-gathering era in books and museums from which she identified what she believed were postures used by shamans. She found approximately fifty such postures that she described in her book *Where the Spirits Ride the Wind*. Using her ritual to induce trance, she had her students stand, sit, or lay in each of these postures while listening to the rattling or drumming.

What she discovered was the postures gave direction to the trance experience in seven different ways. She found that some postures brought about experiences of healing and strengthening. Other postures were for divination or for finding answers to questions. Some postures were for metamorphosis or shape shifting. Then there were the postures for journeying into the three worlds, some for journeying into the lower world, some for this world in which we live, and some for journeying into the upper world. Finally, there were the postures for initiation or for experiencing death and rebirth. Several other postures were for celebration or calling the spirits. All these ecstatic trance experiences facilitate healing, whether personal, for the family, or for the community.

With this discovery, she eventually found land on the Pojoaque Pueblo above Santa Fe, New Mexico where she created the Cuyamungue Institute to research and teach her method of inducing ecstatic trance. On my personal journey into ecstatic trance, I read *Where the Spirits Ride the Wind* and began experimenting with it. I first offered a four morning workshop on ecstatic trance at the 2007 Annual Conference of the International Association for the Study of Dreams and used four of the postures. Being very impressed with how the postures brought about the experiences as Goodman described, I returned to my home in Pennsylvania where I started an ecstatic trance group. I soon read the two books by Belinda Gore,[3&4] a student of Goodman, and found Belinda's email address. She was quick to answer questions that arose on my journey into ecstatic trance and encouraged me to come to the Institute to become a certified ecstatic trance instructor.

With this beginning, from my collection of 4,000 plus ecstatic trance experiences collected from the participants in the groups I have led, during my tenure as the Research Director for the institute, I began writing about where the trance experiences can take a person. First were the experiences that led to healing, as I describe in my book, *The Power of Ecstatic Trance.*[5] Then I realized that beyond healing, the experiences could connect me with my own ancient ancestors, the ecstatic journeys of my book, *Baldr's Magic.*[6] As my journey with ecstatic trance continued and in my travels in Denmark and Sweden, I found that the spirits that arose were stories coming from the Earth of the places I visited. This gave me the stories for my book, *Beowulf's Ecstatic Trance Magic.*[7] The experiences of the groups I hosted then took a turn and were connecting with and healing the Earth: *Trance Journeys of the Hunter-Gatherers.*[8] The next two books were of the ways ecstatic trance could heal others in therapy: *Ecstatic Soul Retrieval,*[9] and *Loki's Children.*[10] My one academic book examines a range of altered states of consciousness, including ecstatic trance as used in psychotherapy: *Applying the Constructivist Approach to Cognitive Therapy: Resolving the Unconscious Past.*[11] My most recent book, *Listening to the Spirits: Surviving the Apocalyptic Age With Ecstatic Trance,*[12] is again of my travels around the world and how the ecstatic experiences of the places I visited connected with the spirits of the hunter-gatherers and their ways of life that were used to heal the Earth from the destruction we as humans have imposed upon her.

I am awed by the number of times the number seven arises, thus, in the next chapter I will elaborate on The Sacred Seven. We will first look to Matthew Wood's[14] journey through the seven stories,

Matthew who began my journey into the seven stories of Genesis, and then the seven chakras of the Kundalini and the seven colors of the rainbow that became a meaningful avenue to understand more deeply the experiences on this journey through Genesis. Also, Gebser's[15] initial five eras of consciousness, but with the addition of two earlier eras, the number is brought to seven, thus adding another dimension to this sevenfold understanding. Finally, I offer my initial and personal journey through the seven stories that clarify the ecstatic postures to be used.

CHAPTER 3

The Sacred Seven

The spiritual number seven in numerology has repeatedly appeared in my writing: the number of the stories in Genesis, Matthew Wood's seven herbs, the number of chakras in the Kundalini, the colors of the rainbow, and the number of eras in my interpretation of the writing of Jean Gebser, *thus*, I considered the number seven important and sacred.

Matthew Wood

The herbalist Matthew Wood's book *Seven Herbs: Plants as Teachers* started me on the journey to write this book. Wood's journey through the seven stories, using his extensive knowledge of both ancient Hebrew, his college language, and the power of medicinal herbs, opened him to the deeper meanings of these stories. I reviewed his book, and because of my review, he asked me to review an early draft of *Seven Guideposts on the Spiritual Path: The Shamanic Story in Genesis.*

These books especially intrigued me because of my deep interest in Nordic mythology and the Garden of Idunn from which golden apples of her tree keep the Nordic Gods and Goddesses young. Because of Idunn and her garden, I often thought to look to the stories of the Bible like the Garden of Eden as ancient myths that reveal deeper meaning rather than the current shallow belief that these stories are literally and historically true. The myths of the world have deeper meanings, often in the language of metaphor. The consciousness of prehistoric cultures was to listen to the spirits of these stories from beyond the rational depth that considers reality as coming only through the five senses of sight, sound, smell, taste, and touch. The ancient myths bring alive these spirits, spirits that gave direction to the life of these ancient cultures.

Matthew's seven selected herbs open us to a deeper understanding of these seven stores that describe a healing journey. Our journey begins when the Lord expels Adam and Eve from the Garden of Eden, a journey that concludes with the story of Joseph who finds heightened spirituality for his return to the Garden. The seven medicinal herbs that provide an outline for Matthew's book give this journey a personal healing dimension. After being passed down orally for many generations, the stories were recorded eons ago during the era of myths, myths written to explain the creation and life on Earth.

Matthew Wood's seven laws of healing describe the dynamics of the healing process. The first three laws are from the practice of Homeopathy, and the remaining four proposed by Matthew are from the earlier version of his manuscript that I reviewed, and though implied, they were not included as laws in his final manuscript:

- The Doctrine of Similars[1]—likes treat likes.
- The Law of the Direction of the Cure[2]–symptoms leave from the inside to the outside.
- The Law of the Healing Crisis[3]—the process of healing needs to pass through a time of crisis while listening to and weathering the crisis.
- The Law of Appropriate Therapeutic Inactivity—on the journey to healing, one's spiritual life needs time to percolate, a time of preparation for giving up and letting go for the spiritual growth process.
- The Law that True Healing is an Art—healing acts require the use of imagination at the well of visionary life to connect us to the spiritual world.
- Law of Appropriate Therapeutic Activity—one needs to grab hold of one's fears in the healing process or for spiritual growth.
- Law of Therapeutic Authority–one needs to accept with

self-confidence the flow of one's inner knowing of that which is true.

These laws take us on the journey through the seven stories with the goal of the shamanic path being union with the spirit without the destruction of individuality. Joseph represents the unification of the three lessons that come before him, letting go, the lesson of Abraham; living in the presence, the lesson of Isaac; and grabbing hold, the lesson of Jacob.[4] Joseph's lesson is that of the authority he gains through his ability to interpret dreams. His ability to listen to the spirits opens the door for his return to the Garden.

Matthew Wood, being an herbalist, identifies seven herbs to facilitate this journey through the six stories to the seventh, the authority and self-confidence of Joseph:

Easter Lily[5]

On this return journey to the Garden of Eden, we begin with Adam and Eve. Like Adam, we begin in a state of innocence at the time of our creation, but soon we find temptation when the snake convinces Eve to eat the forbidden fruit. With our loss of innocence when thrown out of the Garden, we become aware of separating opposites, of that which is good and that which is evil. Though we mean well in trying to do what is right, we require something to protect us from doing evil so God tells us to wear animal skins as a suitable protection from our animal instinct or libido. These animal skins protect us from the dangers of our world.

On the journey towards spiritual purification, spiritual knowledge starts with the realization that we are imperfect and vulnerable to conflicting desires. The cleansing nature of the Easter Lily facilitates us on this journey by cleansing or creating space needed for us to experience and accept these opposites as part of life. The Easter Lily is a flower with a purity of motivation and single-mindedness that it must temper with receptivity to what will happen. We need to not be close-minded but prepared to be open to change. It is a flower of the union of opposites, e.g., happiness and sadness, contradicting opposites we need to experience to become whole.

Matthew Wood offers several examples of how the Easter Lily can open us to accept such contradicting opposites, i.e., the acceptance that the needs for healing require the sympathetic understanding of likes treat likes, the Homeopathic Doctrine of Similarities. From my experience with hypnosis and hypnotic healing this doctrine is equivalent to joining with the client/patient by using the trance inducing language of the "yes-set," i.e., speaking words such that the client will consistently answer, "Yes, that's correct," whether verbally or nonverbally. Wood's case studies are important in understanding this stage of the journey.

Yerba Santa[6]

Next, we meet Cain and Abel, Cain the farmer who sacrifices to God his fruits of the soil, and Abel a shepherd who offers God a blood sacrifice from his flock. Abel lives with his animal instinct, his libido, and though naïve, he is honest to his true self. He wears the animal skins as given him by God. The materialistic and self-cultivating Cain, in his desire to conform to social propriety, works in his fields to impress others with his accumulated wealth. Cain's sacrifice is manmade while Abel's is God made. God does not accept Cain's sacrifice but accepts Abel's. Being jealous of his brother's acceptance, Cain kills Abel. Though Cain denies this murder before God, God hears the voice of Abel's blood crying from the soil. Thus, God drives Cain from the land, causing him to become a fugitive and wanderer. God's purpose is not to save lives but to drive truth to the surface, driving to the surface the self-serving poison in Cain's soul.

The herb that facilitates this journey in driving truth to the surface is Yerba Santa, a remedy for coughs and congestion, driving to the surface the impurities kept in the inner spaces or sanctuaries of the body linings that correspond to the psychic body linings. Yerba Santa identifies and drives these psychic toxins, impersonal psychic garbage, to the surface, thus it follows the Homeopathic Law of the Direction of the Cure, i.e., symptoms leave from the inside to the outside. Matthew Wood describes extensively the signature of the

Yerba Santa and again offers several case studies to show its effectiveness. He notes that Yerba Santa can be helpful when there is some psychic interference, lack of self-insight, or hidden agenda that is obscuring the therapeutic situation. It can be scattered in the four corners of a therapeutic or sacred space.

Iris[7]

The third guidepost, the story of Noah and the Ark, is an example of the third law of homeopathy, the Law of the Healing Crisis, that for healing one needs to pass through a time of crisis. Noah does not point his finger at others, but in his time the world is in a state of spiritual decadence, corrupt and violent, a world that God seeks to destroy with the great flood. God instructs Noah to build an ark, i.e., the self-enclosed totality of the soul, with no windows except on top so that those who survive the flood can only look towards heaven. God tells Noah to take aboard four couples, those of Noah's extended family, and a pair of each animal of the Earth. When the great crisis of the flood subsides and the ark again find's land, God finds Noah acceptable and sets the seven-colored rainbow in the clouds as a sign of his satisfaction and spiritual beauty. From then on, God lets man work to till the land.

Among the signature characteristics of the Iris is its ability to rise above the bog in which it lives, rising in beauty above the crisis of the flood. It is effective in treating the pain of the crises, of the acute reactions that occur in overcoming disease conditions.

So far on this journey, the soul must first open itself to the greater life, which lies beyond its innocence. Second, the soul must follow-through on its spiritual impulses or animal instinct, and third, with the flood, the soul needs to brave the storm of leaving behind old patterns to possess basic spiritual integrity.

Sagebrush[8]

As we continue on this journey to find our spiritual soul, the story of Abraham is the story of recognizing that we are required to let go and experience the pain of sacrifice when we don't get what we want. Abraham and Sarah dearly want a son. Abraham prospers with much land and great wealth, but he needs an heir for all that he has gained. At ninety-nine years of age, after having given up all hope in having a son, the Lord assures him he will have a son. Soon Sarah conceives and gives birth to Isaac. But as a continued test of Abraham's faith, the Lord instructs him to sacrifice Isaac. Abraham takes Isaac to the altar he built on Mt. Moriah, and with his knife wielding hand raised above his son the Lord calls to him to not harm the boy. Abraham then looks up and sees a ram caught in a thicket, a ram that becomes his sacrifice. God blesses them because of Abraham's faith.

To facilitate our own journey through such unwinnable situations, we can find help from Sagebrush. Sagebrush, like other members of the Artemisia family, grows in areas of great devastation, the signature that it is a remedy for the devastations in human life. The way out of an unwinnable situation is to let go of something we initially felt we had to have. On this healing journey, a person needs the empty space or time to percolate on that which is unwinnable before he or she can let it go, i.e. The Law of Appropriate Therapeutic Inactivity. For Abraham and Sarah, there were many years of facing their desire to have children before they let go of the desire, and only then was their desire to have children finally fulfilled. Again, the brief case studies offered add great value to understanding this process.

Cat's Ear[9]

While the story of Abraham was a story of letting go, and we soon will see that Jacob's story is about grabbing on, the story of Isaac is of the balance between letting go and grabbing on. Isaac is contemplative and retiring in seeking spiritual visions. When he is forty years old, his father, Abraham, sends a servant out to the land of his people to find a wife for Isaac, and the servant returns with Rebekah. Isaac and Rebekah lead a prosperous life, but like her mother-in-law, Rebekah too is barren. So, Isaac, at sixty years of age, prays to the Lord for Rebekah, and the Lord grants his prayer. Rebekah conceives and gives birth to twins. Esau, the first born, is Isaac's favorite, and the second is Jacob, the favorite of Rebekah.

To receive spiritual visions, one needs to let go of one's rational mind to allow the images of the vision to come in. The plant Cat's Ear, which appeals to one's imagination, presents the picture of one who turns away from the world to listen to the voice of the spirits. It is a mystical plant. The Cat's Ear, gray and dwelling in the gray of dusk between day and night, brings a person to one's inner awareness. The Law associated with the story of Isaac is that true healing is an art and requires the use of one's imagination.

Black Cohosh[10]

At the sixth guidepost on this journey, Jacob knows to grab onto what he fears, facing what we have formerly hidden from view. Being the second son of twins, at birth, he grabs onto the heel of his elder brother. Being a second son is a disadvantage in dealing with the world. Throughout his life, he finds himself in contentious struggles with his brother, father, wives, concubines, and father-in-law. Late in life when returning from exile to his homeland, as he is about to cross the bordering river, he meets a supernatural being. They grapple, and Jacob grabs on and refusing to let go. The being commands that Jacob let go, but Jacob refuses and responds with "not unless you bless me." He thus receives the blessing that gives him a new name, the name Israel, a name that means "He who fights with God," and he is blessed with the land of Israel.

This story is reminiscent of the story of Beowulf who grabs the arm of the feared Grendel and refuses to let go, an act that eventually ends in the death of this tormenting monster, which leads to Beowulf to become the King of the Geats.

Black Cohosh with its gnarled roots is a remedy for those caught in a state of dark hopelessness and entangled in a web of coercive forces against which they must fight. It is a remedy for the neck pain of a whiplash and for family entanglement struggles. The law offered by Matthew Wood is the Law of Therapeutic Activity, of knowing decisively when to act and when to wait.

Lady Slipper[11]

Finally, we reach Joseph, who wears the spiritual coat of many colors of the seven-colors of the rainbow, the clothing of his soul that represents the highest level of spirituality. The power he gains in his ability to interpret dreams carries him through the painful struggles of life into the new world of the spirits, the return to paradise, the Garden. From birth, Joseph is aware of his spiritual authority. His dreams show him he will have much authority over the land. But to his brothers he is an impractical dreamer, and they feel it is unfair that he does not join them in doing the chores of farming, so they decide to kill him, but Joseph's energy leads them to first sit down to eat. While eating, they see the approach of a caravan and decide they would benefit more by selling him as a slave to the caravan. Because of his ability to interpret dreams he soon becomes overseer of the slaves, but when they arrive in Egypt again jealously leads to him being thrown in prison where he continues to interpret dreams successfully. The Pharaoh hears of Joseph's ability and calls for his advice in dream interpretation, and soon he receives eminent authority over Egypt where he prospers.

The Lady Slipper, a tonic for the nervous system, resembles a slipper and represents that which protects the foot of a wanderer. It suggests that the wanderer settles down, i.e., if the shoe fits, wear it. When in doubt, the Lady Slipper gives you self-confidence that your inner knowledge is true. The law of this seventh guidepost is the Law of Therapeutic Authority, of accepting the truthfulness of what you experience.

The seven herbs identified by Matthew Wood facilitate the journey past each of the seven guidepost stories of Genesis for healing, a process that leads a person into the world of the spirits, the return to Paradise, the Garden of Eden, the Promised Land.

In *Seven Guideposts,* Matthew shows that the self-reflection of imagination, intuition, instinct for truth, and inspiration facilitate this journey. He offers many of his personal experiences of these facilitators, whether from dreams, vision experiences or other life experiences. Such experiences were central in the life of our distant ancestors, to the shamans of the tribes, and now to a few of us who value and practice these facilitators. They help to open us to our dreams and vision experiences such as those offered in trance, whether hypnotic or ecstatic. Matthew selected the seven herbs to facilitate this journey, while I will select seven ecstatic trance postures for the same purpose.

The Kundalini

Again, the sacred number seven greets us, the seven chakras of the Kundalini. But what do the seven chakras have to do with the seven stories of Genesis? We think of the Kundalini as a product of Hindu Yoga, but its origin is much more ancient. As the original homo sapiens-sapiens evolved from the original Eve of Central East Africa, they moved into both West Africa and north into Nubia, and from Nubia into Egypt. The snake of wisdom that wraps the Kundalini was central in the beliefs of the Nubian and the West African, including the Dogon and Yoruba as researched by Edward Bruce Bynum[12] and Laird Scranton.[13] While Bynum described the diaspora of the Kundalini from Africa to India, Scranton's close examination of the sacred symbols of the Dogon of Mali and the Egyptian hieroglyphs uncovers parallel patterns of symbols of the presence of the Kundalini belief in these two ancient cultures. Baba Ifa Karade[14] describes the belief in the Kundalini in the religious concepts of the Yoruba. Karade also relates the seven chakras to the seven colors of the rainbow: red, orange, yellow, green, blue, indigo, and violet. The evidence that the early West Africans migrated across the Atlantic to the Americas, and Luke Blue Eagle's[15] description of the Indigenous Americans connection to the Kundalini, supports this diaspora. Blue Eagle's description and use of gemstones of the colors of the rainbow and the seven chakras for promoting healing is evident in the colors that arise in the ecstatic trance group's experiences and holding the stones have become an important part of my ecstatic trance experiences.

On the Kundalini's journey to India, it passes through the lands of the Canaanites and Hebrews. Though the Hebrews' monotheistic belief rejects the polytheistic beliefs of others of those lands, elements of the Kundalini are evident in the Hebrew and Kabbalah texts. The rising serpent's power of the Kundalini and the biblical Garden of Eden story with the words of the serpent (Gen. 3:5): "In the day you eat of the fruit, your eyes shall open, and you shall be as God, knowing good and evil," reaches to the seventh chakra of the light of supreme knowledge, our Goddess consciousness. But then the Hebrews punished the serpent, relegating it to the lower world, coiled at the root chakra.

The patriarchal Hebrew God is an off-planet God thought to reside in heaven, while for the earlier cultures the Goddess was of the Earth, residing everywhere and within each living being, our Goddess-Consciousness. We need to bring her alive within us as we discover our way back to the Garden, the Promised Land.

As the five of us in the ecstatic trance group journey through the seven stories of Genesis, signs of the seven chakras of the Kundalini appear along the way, often as the colors of the chakras as described by Baba Ifa Karade[16] in his *Handbook of Yoruba Religious Concepts*. These colors were especially useful in identifying where along the spine the members of the group were dwelling in their ecstatic experience.

The Yoruba goals of the seven chakras are told by Karade, goals that pre-date the yogic goals of the Kundalini:

Root Chakra

The Root Chakra brings relaxation to world entanglements, refines the sense organs to reduce confusion and pain, and relieves temporary gratifications. Actions need to be wise with moderation to guard against violent behavior because of insecurities while seeking self-development.

Sacral Chakra

Be observant and study the effect of the moon upon emotions to become free of base emotions such as anger, envy, and greed. A negative mind brings disaster. Guard against over possessiveness and sensual desires, while fulfilling needs for maintaining health. Elevate consciousness for the fine arts and crafts.

Solar Plexus Chakra

Avoid anger, which leads to long-term failure, by reflecting on the consequences of actions. Guard against false pride and the need for recognition, immortality, and power. Seek development of a positive ego and identity, and give to others selflessly, letting love and compassion radiate from within.

Heart Chakra

Develop a higher sense of awareness and sensitivity, emphasizing a sense of purity, innocence, and magnetism. Reflect upon inner sounds and seek to control breathing and heart rate to become independent and self-emanating. Strive for wisdom and inner strength to purify the inner balance of male and female energies.

Throat Chakra

Purify your sound to affect listeners positively and awaken the awareness of eternal knowledge. Reason must overcome the emotions of the heart. Use psychic energy and clairvoyance to communicate without words. Become the master of the entire self, guarding against negative thought while using knowledge wisely. Concentrate on the body's cooling mechanism.

Third-Eye Chakra

Meditate on the third eye to eradicate sins and impurities, revealing the divine within the self and others. For cosmic oneness, practice austerity. Achieve proper balance through spiritual devotion and become one-pointed, seeking to avoid the negative forces that pull one in many directions. Seek the cosmic laws and scriptures that have inner meanings. Rely upon the ability to induce visions of the past, present, and future.

Crown Chakra

Strive to reach the guru within, our Goddess-Consciousness, to attain oneness with all things. Go beyond the illusion of individuality, realizing that the cosmic principles govern the entire universe that you hold within you. Strive to feel the divine and fully realize the divinity within.

Bynum[17] describes the journey of the homo sapiens-sapiens to all corners of the Earth, beginning with the Original Eve of East Africa. He offers evidence of the West Africans' journey to the American continents well before the time of Columbus. Further evidence of this journey to the New World is found in the writing of Luke Blue Eagle.[18] In his book *First Nations Crystal Healing,* he describes the colors of the healing crystals that match the seven colors of the rainbow with energies coming from the seven chakras.

I asked Evan Pritchard whether the first nation people were aware of the power of the Kundalini. Evan Pritchard, a Mi'kmaq author, neighbor and friend in Rosendale, NY, is the director of the Center for Algonquin Culture. He assured me that the belief in the power of the seven chakras was an Algonquin belief, and a belief of the first nation people.

Rising through the seven chakras is rising into the light, to a higher level of consciousness. But this cyclic journey of rising through the chakras is repeated until we reach the highest level of consciousness of attaining the Goddess within in all her fullness.

This repeated journey is the cycle of conception, birth, life, death, and the return to conception and rebirth. Each cycle is of the death of some unhealthy trait and the birth to new health. This cycle of conception begins in the darkness of the womb chakra, the sacral chakra, with the Maiden Goddess carrying the new conception to the crown chakra of the Mother Goddess, our growing Goddess-Consciousness, for birth in the crown's light. Then, as the new life grows into its fullness, the Crone Goddess finds her place in the journey of death with the return to the root chakra of darkness, of the death of another unhealthy trait or issue. From this darkness, it rises to a new conception of a healthier trait at the sacral chakra, rising with the Maiden Goddess to its birth at the Crown's Mother Goddess chakra. This cycle up the spine to the crown chakra and the return to the root chakra is repeated until the highest level of consciousness, our Divine-Goddess-Consciousness within is reached when we join the Universal Goddess-Consciousness. The matriarchal cycle of conception-birth-life-death-rebirth is the cycle to attain one's Goddess identity.

Gebser's Five Evolutionary Eras of Consciousness Now Become Seven

Jean Gebser[21] presents five eras in the evolution of consciousness: the archaic, magical, mythic, rational, and the coming era of time-free transparency. The earliest era, the archaic, began from 160,000 to 200,000 years ago, a time when we lived in a dreamlike state that lasted for many millennia. This dreamlike state was the avenue for the people of the nomadic bands to commune with the spirits from beyond themselves that gave them the direction of how to live. In the process of evolution, this earliest era of consciousness evolved into what Gebser called the era of magic, the era placed in the hands of the tribe's shaman for communing with the spirits. The ancient cave petroglyphs of hunters spearing animals, magical images to insure or facilitate the success of the hunt, is archeological evidence for this magical era of consciousness.

We have little or no evidence of the archaic era, the era in which our hunting and gathering ancestors lived in a dreamlike state. But considering the recognized evolutionary stages of the human brain, breaking down this archaic era into three eras makes considerable sense. The earliest stage was the functioning of the brainstem and the cerebellum, sometimes called the reptilian brain.

The brainstem controls our vital body functions important in our human infancy, the heart rate, breathing, body temperature, and balance. This brainstem era was the time of the dreamlike innocence of our infancy as humans, as we moved automatically through life as directed by the spirits that came to us in our altered state of dreamlike consciousness. This dreamlike consciousness is clear in the story of Adam and Eve.

As our brain evolved, next to develop was the midbrain or limbic brain that opens the person to the brain centers for experiencing emotions. The limbic brain, including the hippocampus, amygdala, and hypothalamus, exerts strong emotional influences on behavior, with emotions that are automatic, pure, and without control. It produces agreeable and disagreeable experiences, emotional experiences caused by the separation of good and evil of when humans gained knowledge by eating the forbidden fruit. This separation is pervasive in life as seen in our language: beautiful vs. ugly, smart vs. dumb, known vs. unknown, me vs. other, us vs. them, etc., separation that creates much of the conflict we experience in life. Most every positive word we use has its negative opposite. As we shall see in the next section, this evolution of the midbrain is central to the story of Cain and Abel, of Cain's behavior triggered by the pure emotion of jealousy.

Third, the evolution of the neocortex, the two cerebral hemispheres of the brain, opens us to the development of language, abstract thought, imagination, and the ability to follow instructions. With the development of interfering language, the voices of the spirits were less likely to be heard. Before, language communication was primarily through signing with hands and body, and in this world of signing the voices of the spirits were more alive. The neocortex is flexible and has almost infinite learning abilities, enabling the development of a human culture that is evident in the story of Noah, of a time of corruption and decadence that brought the flood, and Noah's ability to follow instructions for how to build the ark.

With the addition of these three earlier eras of consciousness we return to Gebser's original four eras that follow the archaic era, first the magical era of the lessons for how to live that come from the visions of the tribal shaman, lessons that bring to the people of the tribe the beginning of their ability to control their emotions.

Next, humans evolved or transitioned into the mythic era of when the mythic stories of creation and life were first recorded in our earliest attempts with the development of language. These recorded ancient myths were metaphorically told by the tribe's bard/shaman, myths that told us how to live, bringing us needed and deeper understanding of emotions and ways to avoid the calamities that arose during earlier eras. These myths, the ancient stories of life, continue to be loved as part of our literary world.

Following this mythic era is the era of rationality in which we have lived for the last 2500 years, the era that has brought us the sciences and modern technology upon which we depend. The rational era grew out of a world restricted to the five senses of sight, sound, taste, smell, and touch. During the rational era, we have concluded that which comes from beyond the five senses, from dreams and other altered states of consciousness, as superstitious or false, and have thought of emotions as distractions from effective living.

Only now as we leave the rational era, as we transition into the era of time-free transparency, are we rediscovering the power of listening to the spirits, the spirits that come from beyond the five senses, the spirits that showed our ancestors how to live. The title of Gebser's book, *The Ever-Present Origin,* reflects this return to the ways of our hunter-gatherer ancestors. The life of these ancient ancestors was automatic as they listened to the spirits that told them how to live. But now, with our new knowledge and deeper understanding of life that grew out of the world of rationality, we can with intent begin our journey into the new world of time-free transparence, a new world that is emotionally alive in the world of the spirits. In this journey into the new era of time-free transparency, we see Joseph with his Coat of Many

Colors and his ability to understand the meaning of dreams as a harbinger of this new era.

My First Ecstatic Journey of the Seven Stories

Adam and Eve

My experience at the time I reviewed Matthew Wood's book began with me standing in the Tlazolteotl Posture from Veracruz, Mexico, a cleansing and healing posture (Fig. 3.1). But soon this Aztec Goddess tells me I should use a divination posture, thus I switch to the Lady of Cholula (Fig. 3.2) from Cholula, Mexico, 350 A.D., which is now in the Branly Museum in Paris. I quickly see an opossum waddling along the edge of a dirt road, alongside a drainage ditch. As I approach it, it seems confused or doesn't know what to do. Should it play dead, or should it run, i.e., waddle away? Since I saw it waddling, it knows that I would not believe that it was dead,

Fig. 3.1

Fig. 3.2

but it cannot move fast. As it waddles away, I follow it for a while and see it disappear into a hole, likely its underground den. I sense it was trying to decide what is right and what is wrong, whether to play dead or to run away.

Cain and Abel

I used the Sami Underworld Posture[24] (Fig. 3.3) found in Lapland, Finland: In my instinct to find the truth, I lie down on my stomach with my arms stretched over my head, and I feel myself diving into a hole in the ground, into an opossum's den, not deep, but it looks cozy with leaves and fluffs of fur. I think it might have been a rabbit's den before the Opossum took it over. She is there with a couple of baby opossums climbing over her. She appears asleep or playing dead. With me there between her and the den's entrance, she is trapped and cannot get out. I poke her with a stick and can see her move slightly, so I know she is not dead. She is in a very vulnerable situation and plays vulnerable to hook my sympathy by looking up at me with her sorrowful black eyes. She seems to know I will not harm her. I appreciate the opossum's ability to eat ticks, ticks which are a big problem in our area. I sense she decides that the most honest or truthful thing to do is to exhibit vulnerability.

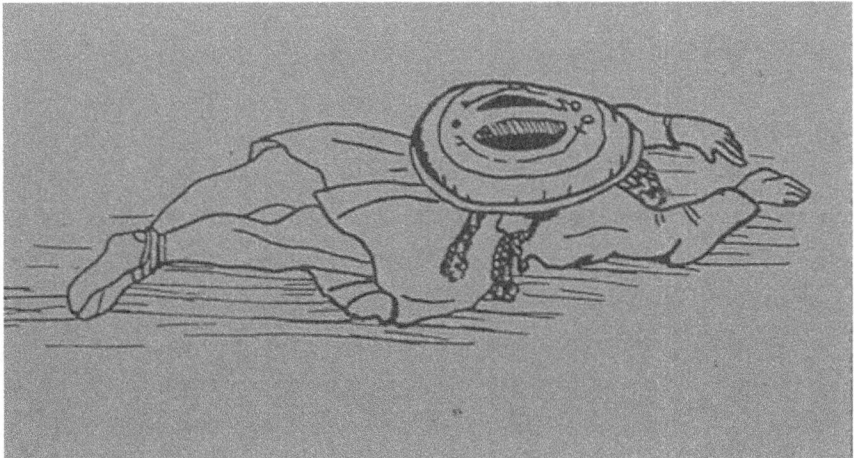

Fig. 3.3

Noah and the Ark

Bear Spirit Posture (Fig. 3.4), late 19th Century, Kwakiutl, Pacific Northwest Coast.

Fig. 3.4

While reviewing Matthew Wood's book, I look back to my earlier experiences to find a Bear Spirit experience I thought fit the story.

To find the strength to face impending disaster, I call upon the Bear Spirit Posture for increased ego strength. As I stand, I can feel the Bear spirit hugging me. I feel increased strength with the Bear's protection. I find myself in the Bear's den, sitting on her lap and nursing at her breast.

I had this experience soon after my diagnosis with prostate cancer. The Bear Spirit became my guide, gave me strength, and nurtured me in getting me through my eventual prostatectomy, a time of crisis. The Bear has become one of my most important spirit guides. As I have learned much from the Bear, I can't consider myself superior to her.

Abraham

At the time I wrote the review of Matthew Wood's book, I used the Feathered Serpent Posture (Fig. 3.5), from Zacatecas, Mexico, 100 to 650 A.D., and it is now in the Los Angeles County Museum. This posture is a death-rebirth or initiation posture.

There are those times in life when we need to sacrifice something dear to us to move ahead in life to find what we want, i.e., a sacrifice that requires letting go. The ecstatic trance posture of the Feathered Serpent, a posture that provides an initiation or death-re-birth experience, is a posture of standing with hands at the waist, a posture that expresses a sense of determination, the determination to let go. I find myself straddling a fast-moving stream of water and in this position, I cannot lift one of my legs back over the stream to the other side to get out of this situation. The water is ice cold and I do not want to go in, but I eventually realize that the only thing I can do is to get wet. The stream is deep enough that I am not sure that it will not wash me down stream or I will fall off balance and into the water, but I let go of my fear and put one foot in the water. It finds the bottom, but I must put my other foot in the water for balance. I then turn and climb to safety. I let go and sacrifice getting my feet wet.

Fig. 3.5

Isaac

With my review of Matthew Wood's book, I used the Calling the Spirits Posture (Fig. 3.6). This Olmec celebration posture is from La Venta, Mexico, from 800 to 400 B.C.

I am standing waiting for the spirits, standing with my mouth open. I stop to think in which direction am I facing and realize that it is to the East. I am

Fig. 3.6

confident that the spirits of the East will come to me to show me what I should do, and sure enough I see the sun rising over the hills and feel the warmth of a new spring day. I go to our garden and dig a shallow trench along one bed and lay a row of lettuce seed, cover it over and pat it down, looking forward to having some early spring lettuce. I feel the spirits telling me it is not too early to plant the seed though we still could have more frost before it comes up. As I sit there next to the newly planted row feeling the warmth of the sun, I see a rabbit hopping across the lawn and know that it too would like the lettuce, so I put row covering of light fabric over the row to protect it though I know it is not much of a barrier for a rabbit. The spirits of the East are giving me instructions for what I must do.

Jacob

To journey with the story of Jacob I used the Jama Coaque Metamorphosis Posture (Fig. 3.7). It is from Northern Ecuador from 500 B.C. to 500 A.D. and is in the Museo Arqueologic Y Galerias de Arte del Banco Central de Ecuador in Quito.

In facing a fear, I use the Jama Coaque Metamorphosis Posture. As I experienced in my book review of Matthew Wood's Seven Herbs, I am hanging onto a rope and feel someone pulling from the other end. I start moving along the rope, hand over hand, to see where it takes me. I cross a small stream and then up a hill to the mouth of a cave. The rope goes into the cave, and I follow it. I soon see a bear at the other end of the rope. He is laughing at me in a good-natured way. I sit down with him and can feel his strength flowing into me.

On another occasion, when using the same posture, I again

Fig. 3.7

hang onto the rope and follow it. It leads me across a river where I see an eagle's nest high in a tree when a feather floats down and lands at my feet. I pick it up and cherish it. I can feel it telling me to rise above my fear as I look up to see the eagle rising in a thermal in the air. I rise above my fear, again my fear of prostate cancer.

Joseph

I used the Lascaux Cave Upper World Posture (Fig. 3.8), found in the Lascaux Cave in France. It is 16,000 years old.

Fig. 3.8

The Lascaux Cave Posture is lying at a 37° angle from the Earth. We use what we call a launching pad, a platform that is at the angle of 37 degrees. I float or easily fly through the sky, above the trees, meadows, and ocean below. It feels so free to fly. The world is at my fingertips. I think of my bucket list of places I want to visit, and I find myself there. I find myself in Lapland among the Sami Reindeer herders among their reindeer, a place I want to visit because from a genome test, I learned that I have a gene that over half of the Sami have.

With ecstatic trance, the stories of Genesis have come alive and personal to me, with personal messages for my spiritual growth, i.e., a return to the Garden of Eden. I will examine these experiences more deeply in the following chapters.

Part II

The Seven Stories Experienced *in* Trance

Each story of Genesis is first told and then followed by the journeys of the five participants, Donna, Lauren, Henning, Lonnie, and me. I will describe the ecstatic essence of these journeys when I summarize the five stories to describe their commonalities and their ecstatic revelations. The ecstatic experiences are told in the present tense to bring them alive in the moment. Each story of Genesis is first retold because some participants did not know or remember the details of the stories.

CHAPTER 4

Adam and Eve

The Story of Adam and Eve

After the creation of the heavens and the Earth, the Lord God formed man from the dust of the Earth and breathed life into him. He put the man in the garden of Eden that was between the Tigris and Euphrates River, commanding him to eat from any tree of the garden except from the tree of the knowledge of good and evil, for in the day that he eats of it he shall surely die.

The Lord brought every beast and bird to Adam who named each. But Adam had no helper fit for him, so the Lord caused him to fall into a deep sleep and took one of his ribs to make a woman. Adam said since she came from man, she should be called woman. They were both naked but not ashamed.

When Eve met the serpent, more crafty than other beasts, it said to the woman, "Did God actually tell you to not eat of a tree in the garden?" She answered, "We eat of the fruit of the trees, but God said, you shall not eat of the fruit of one tree within the garden, neither shall you touch it, for you will die." The serpent said, "You will surely not die, for God knows that when you eat of it, your eyes will open, and you will be like God, knowing good and evil."

So, when the woman saw that the fruit of the tree was good and a delight to the eyes, desiring wisdom, she took of it and ate. She also gave some to Adam to eat, which opened their eyes to the knowledge of good and evil. They knew they were naked, so sewed fig leaves together and made loincloths for themselves. When they heard the sound of the Lord walking in the garden, they hid. But the Lord called to them and said, "Where are you?" And Adam answered, "I heard a sound and was afraid because I am naked." And the Lord asked, "Who told you, you are naked?" Adam said that Eve gave him fruit from the tree of knowledge to eat. The Lord said to Eve, "What have you done?" She answered, "The serpent deceived me, and I ate." The Lord said to the serpent, "Because you have done this, cursed are you and you shall move on your belly, dust you shall eat, and I will put enmity between you and your off-spring and the woman and her offspring." To Eve he said, "I will surely multiply your pain in childbirth. Your desire shall be con-trary to your husband's, but he shall rule over you." And to Adam he said, "Because you have listened to the voice of your wife and have eaten of the tree, it will produce thorns and thistles and you shall eat the plants of the field. By the sweat of your face, you shall eat bread and till the ground from which I created you, for you are dust, and to dust you shall return."

The Lord then made for Adam and Eve garments of skins and clothed them, and said, "Behold, you have become like one of us in knowing good and evil." Therefore, they were sent from the garden, and Adam learned to work the ground which the Lord created. At the edge of the garden, the Lord placed a flaming sword to guard the way to the tree of life.

To journey ecstatically with Adam and Eve, we used the Lady of Cholula Divination Posture (Fig. 3.2), found in Cholula, Mexico, and it is presently found in the Branly Museum in Paris, France. It is pre-Columbian from around 1350 A.D.

Donna

Donna's parents did not go to church. Her Italian father was from a Catholic immigrant family. A bus picked up Donna and her sis-ters on Sundays for a church Sunday School where they read Bible stories about Jesus in paper comic-like books. She hated missing Sunday school because she also got candy there. Her sister said that her parents enjoyed the time away from the children.

Donna did not recall the difference between the Old and New

Testament, but she remembers raising the question of the story of the Garden of Eden, "If everyone came from Adam and Eve, how was there a city with other people to where God banished Cain?" She recalls no meaningful answer, but she remembers the story of Cain and Abel. Also, Eve coming from the rib of Adam made no sense to her. Her affiliation with a church ended when she was 7 or 8 years old.

Journeying with the story of Adam and Eve using the Lady of Cholula Posture, as soon as the drumming begins, I feel myself being carried on a foggy purple/gray current of waves that surrounds me, carrying me west across the central United States. I pause near The Grand Canyon then take a sharp 90 degrees turn counterclockwise to the south, or possibly underground into the earth.

Next, I see a lady squatting on a dusty plain, drawing symbol-like letters or writings in the dirt with a stick. The air is arid. The perspective is through my own eyes, and I see no physical image of "myself." We are in a timeless place, perhaps south of the equator. The lady resembles the statue of The Lady of Cholula and I believe it is the Lady.

She continues to draw equations and diagrams, glyph-like symbols, maybe of constellations and ratios thereof. She instructs me to study things "counterclockwise," opposite of my common perspective, which I perceive as meaning non-geocentric. She tells me to continue to study the stars, alchemy, and the elements.

Holding a long black, white, and brown porcupine quill, she pierces my heart and says it is to let in the light. I feel no pain or discomfort. In fact, I don't believe I have a physical presence in this realm. She says for me to continue working in the worlds between life and death, childbirth, and hospice in an altered-shamanic-state-of- consciousness.

I see colored blooms of purple, then with bursts of yellow and lime green. I hear a whistle, like someone blowing through a reed stalk. She gives me a large round rock to grind grain, and I hear the word "sorghum."

I ask her about my relationship to the Eden story, and she scoffs and laughs, saying, "You know better! You know it is just a remake of the ancient story of RA, the Sun god of the stories of mythology," and she references the Sumerian and Assyrian cultures, saying "You know about the Gods and the Titans," implying that I know too much to be influenced by these later stories. She exhibits qualities of an Elder, stern, unwavering, and authoritative.

Joining Her Ka Body

Donna's journey first carries her into the other world, the world of the spirits, the world of her Ka Body. The Ka Body is a duplicate or spiritual equivalent of her physical body. With no physical sense of herself, and in a non-geocentric timeless world, the counterclockwise world, different from her common perspective shows she is in her Ka spirit body. In this world of alchemy, her internal alchemy is much more personal than the alchemy of turning material substances to gold. This internal alchemy turns her way of experiencing the world to gold. In this shamanic altered state of consciousness, The Elder pierces her heart with a porcupine quill to let in the light, the light of the sun, the Egyptian sun god Ra, bringing her wisdom from beyond her physical five senses of sight, sound, taste, smell, and touch.

Her journey takes her into the purple blooms of the upper chakras that rely upon the strength of her yellow solar plexus chakra, and the innocence of the green heart chakra. When she asks about the Eden story, the Elder tells her that her wisdom is such not to be influenced by these Biblical patriarchal stories, that she knows better. The elder tells her to continue working with the worlds between life, death, and birth in an altered state of consciousness. These worlds are the world of conception in the darkness of the new moon, the darkness of her root and sacral chakras on the maiden goddess's journey of conception as she travels to the world of the mother goddess. The world of the mother goddess at and above the crown chakra brings birth and life into the light with the growing aliveness of her inner Goddess-Consciousness. From this birth and life, she then travels downward in the world of the crone goddess on the return journey of the receding moon, carrying her back into the darkness of the womb chakra, a return to conception and rebirth[1]. This journey of birth-life-death-rebirth is the matriarchal cycle of the mother goddess, the world that the Church has sought to destroy to gain its patriarchal power. We are now seeing a rebirth in the beauty of the matriarchal world, the world in which Donna finds comfort where she finds her Goddess-Consciousness.

Lauren

Lauren, raised Catholic, paid little attention at Mass or Sunday School. Confirmed in the 7th or 8th grade, she got away with learning as little as possible, which seemed fine with the church and her parents. She had some general familiarity with the stories of Genesis but didn't really know the details. She learned the details in our Ecstatic Trance sessions.

As an adult, she considers herself spiritual, but not religious. She stopped attending church when she went to college, but occasionally, when home from college, she went to Mass when asked by her father.

In journeying with Adam and Eve, using the Lady of Cholula Posture, her experience follows:

I am Eve in the garden. I see the snake. There is an apple. Where is Adam? He is an ephemeral figure in this dream. I feel the beat of the drum and slide into the underworld. But what am I doing here? This is a divination posture. Ah, yes, I see snakes in their snake pits. There are so many of them, writhing and twisting within and through each other. The snakes are oneness, but they're dark, cold, and mysterious, living in the dirt. It's not a oneness I want to be a part of.

Why is there only this one snake talking to me? How does he even know about separation, about individuality, given that he's a snake? How is he so much more clever than all the others?

I can feel the warm, soothing dreaminess of the tribe in the garden. This reality is a soft, fuzzy image floating around and through me. I can also feel the cool, stark singularity of leaving the garden. The sun is hot, so bright and clear. I have a choice to make. I love being part of the tribe. This is my home and everything I've ever known. But I want more. What is the promise of this snake, this apple?

I feel and hear the beat of the drum. I'm out in front of my house wearing native leather garb and dancing around the fire. Then I'm alone outside the Garden. But no, I'm not alone but with many others. We are all in a very straight single-file line doing the same dance, but each of us is dancing alone.

This apple feels like all the things we want to possess, all the stuff with which we fill our lives. We work so hard for it because we think it holds some meaning, some prize at the end.

I feel the beat of the drum. I am a ballerina on stage, performing with the drum. My dance is beautiful, lyrical, and staccato all at once. I feel invincible. I am looking for Adam to lift me, but it seems the snake is my partner. He dances upright on his coiled tail, slithering and writhing to my movements. Then I became a flamenco dancer in a beautiful rose dress. I hold the snake up high in a spiral above my head. The snake is holding the apple. I let him slide down my body.

Then I'm back outside the garden. Adam and I are alone; the deed is done. The transition to rationalism doesn't happen all at once. We are still dreamy, but not as warm, not as comfortable. Before, nourishment, safety, and warmth just came, offering themselves to us. Now we seek them out. We use our wits to survive. Slowly, over time, we lose touch with the old ways as the struggle for survival takes over.

As I wrote this, I remembered more about the snake. I saw black snakes in the pit. And the snake I danced with was probably a boa constrictor. I'm not sure which snake I was conversing with. Lonnie in the group mentioned people's fear of snakes. I've had that fear. In part of my trance, I grabbed the snake just below the head and smashed its head. I'm not sure why. Was I afraid of it? Was I angry about the information, the knowledge of good and evil he gave me? I'm not sure where this occurred in the narrative, so I'm not including it in the narrative. But I wanted to include it somewhere to be complete.

Dancing with the Snake

Lauren struggles with seeking the knowledge of good and evil from the tree of knowledge while listening to and valuing the words and wisdom of the snake who offers her more in life, the apple representing her material wants. The Garden where the snake spoke is warm, soft, and dreamy. Lauren has the decision of whether to stay, or does she want more, the logical, dichotomous knowledge of good and evil and to leave? Hearing the drumming with those in native dress dancing in front of the house who are dancing in a straight line feels lonely. Though she is dancing with others in the line, she feels alone in the dance without intimacy. Dancing with the snake in beauty on stage feels invincible and intimate. In her relationship with the snake, her decision to eat of the fruit of knowledge was made without Adam, though Biblically he was with her, and she gave him a bite of the apple.

Matthew Wood, reading the manuscript, questioned Adam's absence. In Lauren's words, Adam was ephemerally with her. If his presence would have been more substantial, he might have interfered with her eating the apple, and the whole course of history would have changed. Thus, Eve committed the original sin by going against the command of the Lord, as did Adam in his sin of standing by his partner but in his own world, uninvolved in the discourse between Eve and the serpent.

By choosing the way of the snake, the source of the wisdom of antiquity, she leaves the garden. The deed is done. She still feels dreamy in the rational world, but she doesn't feel the warmth or comfort of the life in the Garden. Outside the Garden, survival requires seeking nourishment and safety, where she is out of touch with the old ways to survive in the Garden's sustaining Earth. Once outside the Garden, she has Adam to help in their survival. In eating of the tree of knowledge, she finds the way to the world of patriarchy, the dichotomous world of conflict and dissension that we have lived in for the last 2500 years.

Henning

Henning reports he has never been a member of any religious organization. His father was a self-proclaimed atheist, and his mother has always been indifferent to the Protestant Church, which is the predominant religious institution where he grew up in Northern Germany. He had never read Genesis before the ecstatic trance journeys that we did together. His rather limited knowledge of the Bible comes from his study of art history. Beginning in his early 40s (he is now 49) he became intrigued by eastern philosophies such as Taoism, aspects of Buddhism, and Sikhism with his practice of Kundalini Yoga. As for Adam and Eve, and Noah, he had no familiarity other than vague notions gleaned from non-religious popular culture references.

Using the Lady of Cholula Posture for journeying with the story of Adam and Eve was a very cerebral session for me with only a few brief fully immersive moments, though a deep sense of elated relaxation persisted throughout. I have many questions, and few answers come up. I feel the darkness and confinement of the Garden. With expulsion, though now incarnate in a three-dimensional world, all experiences of wo-/man are but a long series of stories on a screen. All is Truth and Truth is in all (Even a lie is truth.) Is all truth sequential or simultaneous, always and forever? Is time real? Is there one truth or many (in parallel universes)? Is there free will or not in Tathātā (suchness or reality)? Has the last word of the Akashic Records already been written?

Did Adam & Eve have a choice over whether to eat the fruit, or did ALL circumstances necessitate the progression of their story (as well as everything else in the world)? However, struggle and felt hardship persists for all of us in the smoke-and-mirrors duality of the world of the "knowledge of right vs. wrong."

A Choice or Not

Though Henning reports that his experience was very cerebral, his experience of relaxation suggests he went into a mild ecstatic trance. The direction of his three-dimensional rationality is on being expelled from the Garden of Eden and the nature of the two worlds, the Garden, and outside the Garden. While the Garden felt confining and dark, the world outside the garden is of struggle and hardship in facing the dualities of knowledge. This transition of struggle brought him several questions, primarily whether it is a choice or a necessity, a philosophical question, another of the dualities that cause the struggle in the world of patriarchy, the world of conflict and dissention through which we have journeyed for the last 2500 years.

Lonnie

Lonnie's ancestry is Jewish. His Jewish grandparents immigrated from Russia and Romania. Though he celebrated his coming of age with his Bar Mitzvah, his Bar Mitzvah education was minimal and without personal meaning. He has not been a practicing Jew in his adult life. Of the seven stories of Genesis, he was minimally familiar with the story of Adam and Eve, and of Noah and the Ark, but not familiar with many of the details of these stories.

> With the Lady of Cholula, I first think of the Garden of Eden and my struggle of being an animal healer vs. controlling nature. In that respect, I go underground in a tunnel, possibly wearing a headlamp, and look up to men trying to control nature with commercial agriculture. Being below ground, I am in the company of soil with the strong smell of earth. There are many healthy worms (snakes) while poisons are leaching into the ground. The last few minutes, all I visualize is the sun coming in and out, warming when out and cooling when in. Also, at some point I see bunches of cells moving together... but that's my scientific mind at work.

The Struggle: To Control Nature or Not

Expelled from the Garden, Lonnie now faces the struggle of the duality of the world outside the Garden. Underground he is with the healthy soil, worms, and snakes, and above ground are controllers of nature and commercial agriculture poisoning the Earth. The metaphoric experience of going underground indicates he has gone into an adequate trance. As a veterinarian, he is much concerned with the health of animals and the Earth. The warmth of the sun suggests that he has some hope for a healthy Earth, the Earth beyond the patriarchal controlling world, the healthy Earth of the Mother Goddess, a spark of life for his Goddess-Consciousness.

Nick

> Using the Lady of Cholula Posture, in my earlier solo experience upon reading Matthew Wood's books, I quickly see an opossum waddling along the edge of a dirt road, alongside a drainage ditch. As I approach it, it seems confused, not knowing what to do. "Should I play dead, or should I run,

i.e., waddle away?" Since I saw it waddling, it knows that I would not believe that he was dead if it plays dead, but he cannot move fast. As it waddles away, I follow it for a while and see it disappear into a hole, likely its underground den.

What Do I Need to Do?

I sense the experience was of trying to decide what is right and what is wrong, whether to play dead or to run away, whether to leave the garden or to stay. I am confused as the opossum, having to decide to play dead (stay in place) or waddle away. It waddles away to a hole in the ground, the way of honesty.

Then, in my second experience with the ecstatic trance group, I first find myself below an apple tree, wondering if I should eat an apple or not. Who do I listen to, the snake or God? I listen to the wisdom within me (whether the snake or God) and think of the Native American way of taking from the Earth, of leaving a gift of thanks. It is not whether I should eat the apple, but it is in the way I eat it, doing it with appreciation and thanks.

Then I find myself in the far North where Idunn is picking the Golden Apples from her garden, the Golden apples that keep the Nordic Gods young. They need the Goddess to keep them young. We need the Earth Goddess to remain healthy. Returning to the Garden is returning to the Goddess.

Who Do I Listen To?

I am expelled from the Garden and must decide between good and evil. "Who should I listen to?" I can have it both ways if I eat the apple with thanks, appreciation and reciprocity, the Native American way. In Idunn's garden we need to listen to her as the Earth Goddess for us to be healthy. In the new world, we live with resolution for the dichotomous struggles by following the healthy ways of Gaia, our nurturing Mother Goddess, lighting a spark of life to bring alive my Goddess-Consciousness. Like each of the others in the group, we have left The Garden and are discovering how to live with that which is good and that which is evil.

For the Group: Finding the Most from Life

Three of us consider the choice of whether to eat the apple and leave The Garden to find more in life. The five of us accept the challenge to study and learn how to live in the world outside of the garden with the knowledge of good and evil. We accept this challenge with a positive attitude in learning how to live in and find support from Nature, our Earth Mother, our Goddess-Consciousness, to live in reciprocity with her, giving back to her as much, if not more, than we take from her.

CHAPTER 5

Cain and Abel

The Story of Cain and Abel

The children of Adam and Eve are Cain and Abel. Cain, the tiller of the Earth, took the fruits of the Earth to the Lord as an offering. Abel, the keeper of sheep, took as an offering the firstborn of his flock. The Lord regarded the offering from Abel but had no regard for Cain's. This angered Cain such that his face fell. The Lord asked, "Why has your face fallen? If you do well, will I not accept you? And if you do not do well, sin is at your door. It is contrary to you, and you must rule over it."

In his anger and jealousy, Cain kills Abel. The Lord asks, "Where is your brother Abel?"

Cain answers, "I do not know, am I my brother's keeper?"

And the Lord responds, "What have you done? The voice of your brother's blood is crying to me from the ground. I shall curse you from the ground so that it will not yield produce in strength for you, the ground which opened its mouth to receive the blood of Abel from your hand. You shall be a fugitive and a wanderer on the Earth."

Cain, expressing his fear says, "This punishment is more than I can bear. Whoever finds me will kill me." But the Lord promised Cain that whoever attacks him shall suffer sevenfold.

Cain then went away and settled in the land of Nod, east of Eden. He and his wife conceived and bore a son Enoch, and they built a city which they named after their son.

*

Before journeying with Cain and Abel using ecstatic trance, a question arose about why the Lord preferred Abel's offering. Cain, as the tiller of the Earth, was doing what the Lord commanded with the expulsion of his parents from the Garden. Abel was wearing the animal skins, like the garments the Lord made for Adam and Eve. To gain wealth as the tiller of the Earth, the labor is great. Sitting on the mountainside tending and protecting a herd of sheep is living in closer communion with the Earth rather than controlling it as with farming. Cain, as a cultivator of the Earth, is materialistic and self-cultivating in his spiritual life with his desire to conform to social propriety. The knowledge needed in farming at the time was more than the knowledge needed to tend a herd of sheep.

Of interest is when the Lord said, "Man has become like one of us in knowing good from evil" is interesting. Does it mean that man's knowledge of good and evil makes man like God? Does what we have learned about the propagation of plants and of farming make us into gods over the land? Herding is more a life of innocence, as was Adam's life in the Garden before eating the fruit. Farming requires greater knowledge, knowing the difference between good and evil, but Cain's desire for the Lord's acceptance leads him to kill Abel, thus evil.

Again, so far, a thread of listening to the Earth runs through these stories, a thread we have lost in our rationality, but it is a thread that we need to regard to regain the path to paradise. According to Matthew Wood[1] "Much of the spiritual activity of the second story of Cain and Abel is of bringing to the surface what

Fig. 5.1

is within us." This suggests the use of an underworld posture, the avenue for listening to the Earth in seeking truth. Looking forward to the remaining five stories of Genesis, the journey back to the Garden of Eden is one of again learning to listen to the spirits of the Earth, to be more like Abel.

Thus, in our journeying with Cain and Abel, we use an underworld posture, the Jivaro Posture[2] (Fig. 5.1).

Donna

> This morning was very stimulating! Using the Jivaro Underworld Posture, I see a dried, open seed pod traveling rapidly downstream on a river. The river leads to a narrowing stream. I notice sandy dark soil. Suddenly a large iridescent scarab-like beetle appears before me, opens her metallic wings, and flies off.
>
> Next, I observe a woman sitting in a tiered courtyard overlooking a babbling brook and garden. She is thin, dark, and regal, wrapped in a sari-like garment. She is reticent and contemplative, and I sense she has a problem she is struggling to solve. The imagery of Egyptian history, Moses and the Pharaoh, as well as male rivalry and the corruption that power can bring, comes to mind. Seeking guidance, she approaches an outdoor altar, a narrow stone gazebo which houses a single statue of a female figure. The area is sunlit, and the colors are golden and sandstone. She is alone and beseeches this Goddess-like statue to help and inspire her.
>
> The next visual is the beetle burrowing underground. The message is to go within, to go dormant, and trust nature. I hear, "14 years." Throughout this experience, I hold no physical presence. It is as if I am watching a movie.
>
> This imagery brings to mind ancient Egypt, Cleopatra and her male contemporaries, Pharaoh, Moses, etc. Also, the 14 years reference seems significant. I thought it might

indicate a planetary cycle, but no obvious correlation shows up, so I will explore other options, like the more literal example of an insect's life cycle.

The Scarab Connects Donna to Nature

In seeking to understand Donna's ecstatic experience, the two influences on her experience, the story of Cain and Abel and her previous experience with Adam and Eve, are important. From her previous experience, she went beyond expulsion from the Garden and into the new world of health and understanding.

A Scarab Beetle, an Egyptian symbol of the rising sun, begins the experience. The head of the Egyptian God of the sunrise has a Scarab head. The Scarab becomes the symbol of resurrection and immortality, worn as an amulet for protection and transformation, a new birth. This transformative new birth was significant in Donna's Adam and Eve experience.

The regally wrapped woman, sitting in her garden overlooking a babbling brook, sat in a contemplative posture suggesting that she was seeking to solve a problem, a problem that Donna senses within her as male rivalry and corruption of power. She goes to her outdoor gazebo with a statue of a Goddess to beseech the Goddess for help and inspiration. The answer comes with the image of the Scarab burrowing into the ground, suggesting to Donna that the answer is to go within and trust nature, to trust her inner Goddess-Consciousness.

The problem of male rivalry and corruption found in the story of Cain and Abel with Cain's jealousy of Abel's herding of animals and being approved by God is an issue we are dealing with in contemporary society. Cain attempts to control the Earth while Abel listens to and trusts nature. The 14 years may be the next 14 years of Donna's life that could bring resolution to this corruption. The dissention we experience within us of the patriarchal world outside the Garden will hopefully be resolved with the return to the Mother Goddess, Donna's Goddess-Consciousness.

Lauren

Using the Jivaro Underworld Posture, at first, nothing happens. Then, suddenly, I slip down into the underworld. This is the world I inhabit. I am Persephone, Queen of the Underworld. My home is comfortable. It is dark, cavernous, and damp, but spacious and surprisingly clean. A fire in the enormous fireplace adds warmth and light.

I greet Abel as he arrives in the Underworld. The wound from the blow to his head causes him to be disorientated. He vaguely understands that his brother caused his death, but that doesn't really make sense to him. I hold Abel and offer him comfort. He lies down on a bench with his head in my lap. My job is like that of a temple priestess. The hell of the middle world is from where I greet people. I comfort them and help put their bodies, hearts, and souls back together. I give Abel tea and prop him up near the fire. When I am sure he is in decent enough shape to be on his own, I leave to greet Cain, who has just arrived.

Cain is waiting and despondent. He doesn't understand why Abel's gift was superior to his own, why God would pit them against each other, and why God would kill him— although he has remorse for killing his brother. I hold him while he weeps. I tell him he is safe here.

Amid this activity, I, as Lauren, have had images of myself as one with the underworld. I become a molecule of dirt in the cave, then the whole cave, then the whole underworld. I know myself as distinctly me, and as part of the underworld, including Abel, including Cain. I don't understand this God who pits brothers against each other and wonder why he prefers one gift to the other. And then I realized, "Why?" is the wrong question. There is no place for that here. Only oneness exists here. There is no separation in the underworld where the God of separation does not exist.

I take Cain's hand and we dance, a slow folk dance like is done in Sweden. It's usually danced with a group in a circle, but Cain and I dance it alone. The slow, repetitive, rhythmic movements soothe Cain. Eventually, I invite Abel to dance with us.

I, as Lauren, have an image of my friends here dancing this dance out front of my house outside around the fire pit in the front yard. It is beautiful and peaceful, all of us moving as one. I put my arms around Cain, and Abel stands behind me, putting his arms around me. After a while, I moved away. Abel and Cain hold each other, and I stand behind Abel with my arms around him. Cain weeps, and his tears heal Abel's wounds. Then we shift around again. This time I'm behind Cain, with my arms around him. My love and Abel's love heals the separation within Cain. Then the drumming stops.

Queen of the Underworld

Lauren, as Persephone, Queen of the Underworld, greets Abel and Cain to promote the healing of their separation. In asking why God would promote such separation, she realized that "Why?" is the wrong question. As Queen of the Underworld, she is one with all that is of the underworld, the particles of dirt, the entire underworld and all who live there. There is no separation in the Underworld.

Lauren finds herself beyond the world of separation, beyond the world outside the Garden. Her underworld is the Garden, the world of innocence, the matriarchal world of the hunter-gatherer where she finds healing with the rebirth of her Goddess-Consciousness. Outside the Garden is the world of the dichotomies of rationality, the world of conflict and strife, but as we enter the new Era of Time-Free Transparence as described by Jean Gebser[3], we find that the world beyond the rational is a world of innocence without the conflict caused by the dichotomies we face each day, beyond separation. It is the world of the Garden, the world of Lauren's Goddess-Consciousness.

In this new world, Persephone tells Cain and Abel that they are safe. Here there is no God of Separation. She dances with the two brothers, bringing them together. As she leaves them to hold each other in the dance, Cain's tears heal Abel's wound in this world of Gaia.

Henning

I used the Jivaro Underworld Posture. The brothers are the offspring of Adam and Eve, and the serpent, in its wisdom, foresees their story, as it does all stories. Cain and Abel, as for all of us, do not possess the serpent's wisdom, and they must live through their story to gain insight for themselves. The brothers are two sides of an energy exchange. Cain's murder of Abel results from his fear of not having enough. He toils in the fields for fear of not having enough food, and he slays Abel for fear of not getting enough of God's love. Fear literally turns his heart into stone, and he tears his stone heart out of his chest and smashes Abel's head in with it. Abel is an energy field (like all "solid matter") and absorbs the blow, his material form is destroyed. He takes the blow with grace, love, and forgiveness for his brother as he recognizes that he, too, has shed the blood of fellow creatures, the sheep of his herd.

*

An older man takes off his jacket and gets comfortable in a lawn chair on a Brooklyn rooftop. He is Abel, bearing the mark of the stone on his own heart, which has turned him into a participant of the inner-city rat race. He is unaware of the web of life of which he is a part. He closes his eyes, and the potted plants that surround him engulf him with caressing branches, vines and leaves as he falls asleep feeling well nurtured, yet he remains unaware of the floral source of his momentary contentment.

Separation

Henning comes to the story of Cain and Abel rationally, under-standing knowledge as we understand it now, knowledge gained through experiencing the serpent's wisdom of foresight, of knowing what life will be like outside the garden when Adam and Eve lose their innocence and make judgements about life, about good and evil. The energy exchange of their two sides of knowing good from evil is evident in their story, of Cain's fear of not having enough, fear that he imparts upon Abel by smashing him on the head with his stone heart.

As with Donna's experience of the two bodies, the physical body and its duplicate, the spiritual or Ka body, Abel passes from his physical body of solid matter to his spiritual body, taking the blow with grace, love and forgiveness. He knows that the blood shed by his butchered sheep speaks from their Ka body.

This realization takes Henning into a deep trance experience of being Abel comfortably sitting in a lawn chair on a Brooklyn roof-top. The mark of the stone on his heart places him in the inner-city rat race like the rat race of Cain's enterprise of farming the land, of trying to get ahead in life. But, going into his Ka dreamworld he experiences the nurturance of nature as he did as a sheepherder, being caressed by vines and leaves. Thus, Abel learns deeply by experiencing the separation of the two worlds of good and evil in his journey to recover his Goddess-Consciousness.

Lonnie

I am well rested today as I use the Jivaro Underworld Posture. I cannot rest my mind this morning. The five min-utes of meditation do not help. The drumming starts and I feel heavy in the posture. My left arm and my right hand on my forehead feel very heavy. I feel a smack on the side of my head. I open my eyes and look around. The drum-ming continues. I close my eyes and I drift off, again feeling a smack on the side of my head. I'm alert, open my eyes and look around. When the drumming stops, I close my eyes and drift off.

A Smack on The Head

Though Lonnie complained he could not quiet his mind, he went into a very deep trance as shown by the experience of the heaviness of his arms and hand, and of not remembering his trance experiences between the times he "drifted off" when he closed his eyes and experienced the smack to his head.

For me to understand his trance experiences, I went into a trance as I read his reported experiences. When I go into a trance with someone else, and now, while reading someone else's experience, I find my depth of trance is that of the other person. Here, I found myself not remembering my experiences because of the depth, but before experiencing the smack to my head I had the flash of Cain smacking Abel on the head, a flash that suggests that this is what Lonnie experienced during the episodes of amnesia. The smack brought his attention back to the present, lifting him out of the deep trance. In my experience, when smacked on the head I saw stars, stars at my crown chakra, stars of enlightenment.

Knowing a bit about Lonnie's philosophy of life, of being a veterinarian and vegetarian, he would be appalled with the thought of killing someone or any life. Thus, I expect he was not ready to experience Cain killing Abel. Feeling the love for all life and refraining from killing opens Lonnie to the love of the Mother Goddess, his internal Goddess-Consciousness.

Nick

In reporting my two Cain and Abel ecstatic trance experiences, my first solo experience was at the time of my review of Matthew Wood's book. I used the Sami Underworld Posture (Fig. 3.3): In my search for the truth, I lie down on my stomach with my arms stretched over my head in the posture. I feel myself diving into a hole in the ground, into the opossum's den, not deep but cozy looking with leaves and fluffs of fur. I think it might have been a rabbit's den before the opossum took it over. She is there with a couple of baby opossums climbing over her. She appears asleep or playing dead. With me there between her and the den's entrance, trapping her so that she cannot get out, I poke her with a stick and can see her move slightly. I know she is not dead. She is in a very vulnerable situation and plays vulnerable to hook my sympathy by looking up at me with her sorrowful black eyes. She seems to know I will not harm her. I sense she decides that the most honest or truthful thing to do is to exhibit her vulnerability.

The World of Vulnerability

My focus on this first Cain and Abel experience concerned having to decide between being alive or the dishonest response of playing dead while living in the world of dichotomies, the world of separation. While trapped, being alive and showing feelings of vulnerability were most effective and honest. Living in the world of dichotomies and separation is a world of vulnerability, as is so evident in our present world. Letting myself feel this vulnerability is the solution for dissolving the separation caused by this dichotomy.

My second ecstatic experience is with the ecstatic trance group, using the Jivaro Underworld Posture (Fig. 5.1). I am looking at a deer hide I am preparing for a drumhead. It is soaking in wood ash and water to remove the hair. I am then standing where the deer died with its blood soaking into the ground. I go underground below this blood, and I watch it soak deeper and deeper as it comes towards me. Then I think of the blood of Abel that spoke to the Lord from the Earth.

Returning to the hide for the drumhead, I look forward to completing the drum so I can beat it to honor the deer that died. I will take the drum to where the deer died and beat it to honor the deer, and each time I use it, I will think of the deer that sacrificed itself to the hunter. Its blood enriches the soil.

I then come back to our compost bins. I have great intent to enrich the soil with the compost I am making from the invasive weeds and the horse manure from Lonnie. I feel that what I am doing differs from the farming of Cain in that I give back to the Earth the compost that feeds the worms and other microorganisms to enrich the soil. I value the Earth for what it provides, and I do not take from it in my greed for wealth. At least I hope so, though I know I do not know everything and make mistakes.

The Blood of the Earth Speaks
In the second Cain and Abel experience with the group, I experience the deer's blood calling from the Earth like God hearing the blood of Abel calling from the Earth. The deer's blood and the compost are to enrich the soil. I have been called to honor the fertility of our Earth Mother by returning to her that which I take, honoring her with reciprocity of giving back to her as much, if not more, than I take.

Resolution of the Violence and Conflict of Separation

The experiences of each of the five of us sought resolution to the violence, conflict and suffering caused by gaining the patriarchal knowledge of good and evil. We found the resolution to overcome the dichotomies with which we live by again living with nature and venerating our Earth Mother in our Goddess-Consciousness.

CHAPTER 6

Noah and the Ark

The Story of Noah and the Flood

After many generations, the Lord saw that the wickedness of man was great. The Earth was corrupt, filled with violence and corruption of the flesh. Noah, though, was a righteous man, blameless in his generation, and walked with God. God, determined to end all flesh, instructed Noah to build the ark, giving him very specific instructions in how it should be built and to take aboard his wife, his sons, and their wives, and a male and female of all breathing life, whether clean or unclean, along with enough food for all to save them from the flood. The rain fell for 40 days, covering the Earth, and blotting out everything that breathed, and the flood covered all the high mountains under heaven for 150 days.

Noah's eyes were not deflected by the corruption. He kept his eyes on the Lord. There were no windows in the ark except upward to heaven. Then God made a wind to pass over the Earth, restraining the rain. The water decreased, and the ark came to rest on Mount Ararat. After ten months, the tops of the mountains again appeared. Noah sent forth a dove to see if the waters abated from the ground, but the dove returned having found no place for its feet. After another seven days, he again sent forth the dove, and it returned with an olive leaf in its beak. Then, after another seven days, Noah sent forth the dove, and it did not return. So, Noah removed the covering of the ark, and the Earth was dry.

God said to him "Go Out," and Noah built an altar to the Lord and took some of every clean animal and bird for a burnt sacrifice to the Lord. The Lord said, "I will never again curse the ground because of the evils of man. While the Earth remains, seedtime and harvest, cold and heat, summer and winter, day and night shall not cease," saying to Noah and his sons, "Be fruitful and multiply and fill the Earth. Every moving thing that lives shall be food for you, and as I gave you the green plants, I give you everything." Also added to this covenant was one condition: "Whoever sheds the blood of man, by man shall his blood be shed, for God made man in his own image." The rainbow of seven colors became a sign from God of this covenant.

Then Noah, being a man of the soil, planted a vineyard. But he drank of the wine, became drunk, and Ham, his youngest son, and the father of Canaan, found him lying naked in his tent. The other two sons covered him, walking backwards so as not to look upon their father's nakedness. Learning this, Noah's curse on Ham was that he would become a servant to his older blessed brothers.

*

As we begin our journey with Noah, we will learn to rise above our materialistic and selfish ways, acquiring the beauty of our internal spirituality. We selected the Bear Spirit Posture because it provides the needed centering strength to face potential crises and addictions without going astray. Again, we start with Donna as we examine her Bear Spirit Posture (Fig. 3.4) experience, a healing and strengthening posture.

Donna

With Nicholas's gentle guidance, I prepare for my Noah/ Bear experience at home, using the Bear Spirit Posture (Fig. 3.4).

I begin by lighting a piece of sweetgrass. Next, in my attempt to locate a drumming CD amid my half-unpacked household, as if waiting for me, my hand locates a small chunk of bear root given to me in a sweat lodge several years ago. As I bite off a piece and chew, I sense a shift and sit quietly for several minutes. With heightened awareness, I easily locate my medicine pouch and see my single bear's claw resting on top. I hold this claw in my left hand and further sense the bear near me. An appropriate CD appears with no effort, Sacred Drumming by David and Steve Gordon. I use the first track named "The Four Directions," a five-minute track to call the directions. Loosely holding the directions, I allow the music to do the work as I soften and deepen my breath. Next, I cue up the Guardian Spirit, and Return Journey tracks, which totaled 15 mins, and I assume the posture.

I am Bear as I emerge from hibernation into a bright grassy field. It is springtime, sunny, breezy, and cool. I sense flowers and blooming grasses and seem to be somewhere in the far north. Feeling playful and happy, I, as Bear, smell the dirt, and with my heightened sense of smell, I sniff the air and everything around me. From this point on, I identify as Bear.

My skin, loose and light, moves smoothly over my bones. Quickly my life passes by, and I sense a fast-forward day/night cycle, experiencing a sped-up bear lifetime. Next, I am only bones, a skeleton which is used to make a musical instrument, a drum perhaps. Now, aware that I am connected to everything while still being strongly "bear," I experience the stars, Ursa Major specifically. Amid a deep knowing that the stars offer guidance, my sense of bear deepens. I feel my teeth and mouth dripping with saliva.

My brother Salmon appears jumping upstream in mass. We are one-and-the-same and live in unity.

Now, with a shift in consciousness, I ask, "what about Noah and the Ark?" I am myself consulting with Bear. Bear explains we forgot our connection. The story is a metaphor to remind us to stay connected not only to innocence and strength but also to the cosmos, the waters, and all life.

I ask for personal healing and am cloaked in a full, furry, black-brown bearskin with a head attached. Bear instructs me to attend to my nervous system. Take B vitamins and strengthen my pelvis and core with swimming and yoga. I ask Bear to stay with me for strength and guidance, and Bear agrees, and the session ends.

As soon as I begin transcribing my Noah/Bear experience, I see how it relates! I am both Noah and Bear, emerging into a new world, or the same world, but with a new understanding and appreciation for all life and our place in it. My love for dirt was a potent factor and comfort for both me and Henning. God, the Cosmos and Bear are interchangeable. Our guide is a benevolent yet ordered higher power that creates, even as we too co-create. So interesting!!

Bear Becomes Donna's Guide to Reconnect with Everything

Donna becomes Bear, coming out of hibernation with loose skin who quickly goes through the lifetime of the bear and becomes bones. She still is strongly Bear, the Ka body or spirit body of Bear, and she connects to everything, including the stars, specifically Ursa Major, that offers guidance to her deep sense of Bear. She recognizes she is part of everything, of all life, including her brother the Salmon. We are all one.

As Bear, she recognizes that we have forgotten our connection to everything, and Bear teaches us to stay connected, including our connection to the cosmos, the water, and all life. In her healing, Bear cloaks her in bearskin with head attached and instructs her to take care of herself with what she eats and how she exercises. Bear agrees to stay with her as her guide when she asks.

This experience relates to the Noah story as Noah/Bear emerges into the new world or the same world, but with new and deeper understanding, appreciating all life and our place in it, loving the dirt as Bear loves the dirt. God, the Cosmos, Gaia, and Bear are one. We are the co-creators of everything. The corruption that brought the flood is our disconnect to everything. Donna reconnects with the oneness of all life, of our Mother Goddess who has created everything, bringing alive her internal Goddess Conscious.

Lauren

At first, with the Bear Spirit Posture, I was Noah, lying drunk in my tent, feeling the room, the world, spin around me. Ahh, the pleasure of wine. The intoxication is so delicious until it is not. This feeling, whatever it is, is part of the world the shaman inhabits, dreamlike and flowing. It's the opposite of the rational, orderly, and controlled, the everyday world we inhabit. The shaman lives in both worlds, going to the dreamlike place and then bringing back its gifts to the rational world. The shaman must walk a very fine line, embracing the pleasure of the dream world but knowing when to leave. Getting lost there is like the members of God's world getting lost in the pleasures of the flesh.

I am the bear in the posture, protecting my young, protecting my person. As I lumber along, I feel the shifts in weight between my right and left foot as I step, and the shifts between my opposite shoulders. The bear, naturally and gracefully, straddles the line that the shaman walks, leaning to one side and then the other. It's not about staying on the line. It's about walking a little to the left, a little to the right, never straying too far from the center.

I feel myself as the snake, whose body is a line, yet who is as incapable as the bear of staying on the line. The snake must curve left and right, back and forth, repeating S curves, simply to move. The snake is not slithering along the line, but is always a little to the left, a little to the right.

Then I am an ape, lumbering similarly to the bear, weight rolling from my right hip to left, each step supported by the shoulders, arms, and knuckles of each side. As the ape I walk for a while, then pause and stare, observing my surroundings, appreciating the power and heaviness of my body. My head is clear, my breath is slow. Eventually, the spark of light and energy that is me leaves the ape, which collapses to the ground like a discarded Halloween costume.

Back to Noah and his sons, back to all those people god punished and killed, who didn't understand the line between the rational and the dream world. Noah, when he built the ark, didn't understand the dream world. He was rational, controlled, and obedient to God. After he grew his grapes, he became curious about the pleasures of the flesh. He led a dual life, so proud of his favor with God, so proud of his steadfastness, his righteousness. And yet, he was curious. He drank the wine, got drunk, and got lost in the dreamworld.

Noah's son Ham was aware of Noah's pride and judged him for it. Ham found Noah naked and drunk and told his brothers, mocking his father. Noah was deeply ashamed of his own behavior and was furious with Ham for mocking him to his brothers, so Noah punished him. Ham was to become a servant to his brothers.

Ham's brothers knew not to look at their father, willing to forego Ham's knowledge to avoid Noah's punishment. The brothers were kind to Ham. They allowed Ham to serve them as the Lord decreed, but they were just.

The Line Between the Rational and the Dream Worlds

Noah overstepped the line between the rational and dream worlds with his drunkenness in finding the pleasure in drinking his brewed wine. Finding this line takes practice. Other species, the back-and-forth lumbering of the bear and ape, and the slithering path of the snake, naturally straddle this line, never straying too far from the center. Noah's obedience to God opened the door to growing grapes and becoming a brewer, opening him to experience the curious and pleasurable world of the spirits, a world in which he initially got lost, bringing him shame in the eyes of his sons. The lesson of this shame brought him to find an appropriate balance. Those killed in the flood did not understand this line between the two worlds. Lauren's new understanding of this line brings her to oneness with all life, with our Earth Mother, her Goddess-Consciousness, whether the bear, snake, ape, or the way of the shaman.

Henning

I was very shaky and uncomfortable standing in the Bear Spirit Posture, which is likely because of having served myself rapé snuff before the experience, an experiment I don't care to repeat, in all honesty.

I am the dove. Released the first time, strong winds pick me up and take me high, high above the ark and the sea. I battle the gale. I see no land beneath me, far and wide, and I return to Noah's hands. I trust him deeply.

Inside the ark it is dark and the light coming in through the door blinds all. I tell all creatures to be patient. My mate comes next to me and, as do the other animals around me, relishing the salty sea breeze I carry into the fetid ark. My mate cleans my feathers with her beak.

After a week, I go out again and find some recent growth on the wet and slimy ground. I eat fresh greens to my heart's content and bring back a sprig for my mate. There is a new life, a new chance at life waiting for all of us, so be patient.

I go out again, feeling miserable and afraid of an uncertain future that has no marks on anything familiar, nothing but newness. To comfort myself, I wallow in the dirt, over and over, taking dust baths.

After the Flood

When the rain stops and the flood waters recede, the Dove looks to the new world. On his second venture off the Ark, he finds new growth of greens to eat, and on his third venture he finds dry land, but he feels miserable and afraid with the unfamiliarity of the new world, though he finds the dirt to take a dust bath.

This new world, without human or animal life other than that on the Ark, is an unfamiliar but a new beginning, and what will it be like? So far, each person of the group sees this new world after the flood from a different perspective. Donna sees its beauty in discovering the interconnection between everything of Mother Earth, while Lauren sees it as a time to learn the balance between the rational and the dream world. In the old world, the people were corrupt in their addiction to the ways of the flesh. Now, Henning experiences fear because of the lack of familiarity with everything new in the world. Let's see what Lonnie must add to this picture. Henning's emotional response of experiencing fear is the way of the matriarchal world, and not the patriarchal response of denying emotions in the attempt to control and maintain power over life's experiences in the world of rationality.

Lonnie

First, while standing in the Bear Spirit Posture, I am Noah, then I am not. I am now Noah's animal helper. It is very hot. The world is burning. The ark, made of wood, is smoldering. There are people but they don't appear normal, but zombie-like. They all have a very anxious look on their faces, very agitated. The other species appear calm. You can see it on their faces. They are entering the ark in an orderly fashion. I am pleased to see some of my favorites. The pigs show up, and I welcome them aboard. It is getting hotter, and time slips by. There are fires all around us, and the people are melting. The ark is now metal and becomes a rocket ship. The hatch closes, and we take off into space. We watch from above as the earth burns. My wife and I oversee all the animals. We clean and feed them and make sure they are comfortable. Noah then tells us that the fires have ended, and we can return to earth. We land and depart the ark. We see the burned land, but we also see new plant growth. There are a few people around, but they are calm and welcoming.

Welcoming Survivors

Lonnie, as Noah's helper with the animals, left the burning Earth in a rocket. When the fire ended and the rocket returned to the Earth, the world was calm with welcoming survivors. Each person in our group comes to the Noah and the Ark story, focusing on different parts of the story. Donna, as with her earlier experiences, focuses on a new life beyond these stories. Lauren focuses on Noah's life after the flood of growing grapes and making wine. Henning focuses on the end of the flood with the Dove leaving the ark to see the condition of the Earth. As the flood recedes, Lonnie, upon return, finds the survivors welcoming and calm. Entering the new world, the matriarchal world of the Mother Goddess, feeling welcomed and at one with all life, brings alive Lonnie's Goddess-Consciousness. My two experiences with the Noah story will add another perspective.

Nick

My first ecstatic trance experience with the Noah and the Ark story was at the time I reviewed Matthew Wood's book. I looked back to my earlier experiences to find a Bear Spirit experience I thought fit the story.

To find the strength to face impending disaster, I call upon the Bear Spirit Posture for increased ego strength. As I stand, I can feel the Bear's spirit hugging me. The Bear Spirit is protecting me, and I feel stronger. I find myself in the Bear's cave, sitting on her lap and nursing off her teat.

I had this experience soon after my diagnosis of prostate cancer. The Bear Spirit became my guide, gave me strength, nurturing me in getting me through my eventual prostatectomy. The Bear has become one of my most important spirit guides. As I have learned much from the Bear, I cannot consider myself superior to the Bear.

My second experience was with the group. I first felt the

rising strength within me of the Bear Spirit, strength for me to face life's crises. Then I was the two wolves from that last time I did the Bear Spirit Posture as they crept towards the bonfire. I could see their glowing eyes in the dark, and then, as they got closer to the fire, I could see their beautiful gray fur. I felt love towards them. Then I went to a much earlier Bear Spirit session where a cougar was coming towards me, and I again felt the same loving feelings.

Where are the Crises in my life?
About twenty years ago, while lying in bed in the morning, the thought came to me: Could I still call myself a Christian since I could no longer accept a creator God who would have a chosen people among those he created, or an off-planet god whose creation was not heaven, but heaven was a place that people would long for after death? This evolution in my thinking was gradual, and this thought was not a crisis but an opportunity, opening new doors to my world of the spirits.

Then I thought of when I was told I had prostate cancer. After a few moments of shock, I asked in curiosity why I have cancer and thought of it as an opportunity. Then when moving to New York from Pennsylvania where I had forty years of close ties that were so much part of me, again I saw it as an opportunity, surprising my wife how easily I accepted this change.

Then I realized that there are no crises in my life with my belief in the Great Mother Earth who provides the power of spirituality within me. I felt very relaxed and enjoyed the vibrations of the drum as the heartbeat of the Earth, an experience of basic spiritual integrity.

Crises Provide Opportunities

Facing the crises of the flood caused me to face the various crises in my life, crises that I experienced as opportunities that brought about healthy change. In examining the similarities between the experiences of each of the five of us, each experience provided a door to change, a door into a new world, each from a different perspective. My experiences followed suit, but from the perspective of facing the crises in life as opportunities. The others in the group found the changes in life by looking at different aspects of life before and life after the flood. But each found in the story of Noah as an avenue for change in the new world. Donna appreciated the interdependency of all life. Lauren recognized the need to be responsible in the new world, of not getting lost imbibing in all its pleasures. Henning was anxious about the lack of familiarity with what he found in the new world, and Lonnie appreciated being welcomed. The differences we experienced are important to our personal growth, but also important considerations for entering the new world. My experiences in finding the strength to face crises in my life are a loving and healing strength that comes from our Mother Goddess, not from the conflictual way of life as we have experienced with the patriarchal God.

CHAPTER 7

Abraham

The Tower of Babel

Before the story of Abram, which comes next, is the story of the Tower of Babel. According to Julian Jaynes, the people initially heard the voice of the Lord as if coming from beyond themselves. But with evolutionary changes in the structure of the brain, they no longer heard the voice of the God, so they tried to reach God by building a tower.

Matthew Wood, in his reading of this manuscript, notes that the chronology of these events is wrong according to Genesis: 11. As the people journeyed from the east, they settled in the land of Shinar where they made bricks to build a city and a tower whose top reached unto heaven. They, presumptuously speaking as God, spoke with no restraint, "let us make us a name." So, the Lord, hearing this, scattered them abroad, and they spoke different languages and did not understand one another.

Still, the nature of the language of the seven stories changed after the story of Noah. As Julian Jaynes explains this change, the voice of God came from the left hemisphere of the brain as if it came from outside the person. At the time of the Tower, the people did not hear the voices in this way. The voice of the Lord was now experienced in visions, dreams, and visions of angels of the Lord coming from within oneself.

The Story of Abraham

The Lord said to Abram: Go from your country, your kindred and your father's house to the land that I will show you. I will make of you a great nation and will bless you, and your name will be great.

Abram was 75 years old when the Lord appeared to him. So, Abram took with him Sarai, his wife, and Lot, the son of Haran, his brother, and they went into the land of Canaan. The Lord again appeared to him and said, "I will give this land to your offspring". So, he answered by building an altar to the Lord. In a later vision, as we shall see, when Abram was 99 the Lord came to him and gave him a new name, Abraham, and Sarai's new name, Sarah.

There was a severe famine in this land, so they went on to Egypt. There he feared for his life because of his wife's beauty, fearing someone would kill him for her, so he called her his sister. When the Pharaoh took her, a great plague afflicted the people of Egypt. Blaming Abram for the plague, he returned Sarai to him and sent them away. So, they returned to the land of the Canaanites.

Abram had sheep, oxen, donkeys, camels, and servants. He and Lot both had great wealth but insufficient land for both to dwell together. So, Abram told Lot to take the land he wanted, and he would take the other. Lot saw the beauty of the Jordan Valley so journeyed there and they separated with Abram settling in the land of Canaan. The Lord told Abram that this land was his and his offspring, so Abram again built an altar to the Lord.

There was great strife in the land of Lot, and the King of Sodom and Gomorrah took Lot as a captive along with all his wealth and family. Abram, hearing this, took up arms against the enemy of Lot and rescued him, bringing his wealth and family back to Canaan. When peace came to the Valley of the Jordan, the new king asked for Lot's return, so Abram sent him and his wealth back to the Jordan Valley.

Another vision came to Abram that the Lord would protect him, but Abram said to the Lord, "What will you give me for I am childless and have no heir for the land." The Lord told him he shall have an heir, and that his seed will be as the number of stars in the heavens. He questioned the Lord, how am I to know that I am to possess this land? The Lord asked for several animals to be sacrificed, and Abram brought them to him. Then Abram fell into a deep sleep and in the darkness the Lord said, "Know for certain that your offspring will be sojourners in the land that is not theirs and will be servants to the Canaanites for four hundred years. But I will bring judgment on the nation that they serve and afterward they shall possess great wealth on the land from the Nile River of Egypt to the Euphrates."

Since Sarai had borne Abram no children, she offered him one of her servants, Hagar, to provide him with a child. When the servant conceived, she looked with contempt at Sarai, so Sarai dealt harshly with her, and she fled. An angel of the Lord found Hagar and told her to return to Sarai and submit to her, telling her that her son shall be called Ishmael. He shall be a wild donkey of a man, fighting against everyone, and he shall dwell over and against all his kin. Abram's age was 86 years.

When Abram was 99 years of age, the Lord told him he shall be the father of a multitude of nations. "No longer shall your name be Abram, but you shall be called Abraham, and you will be exceedingly fruitful. I will give to you and your offspring all the land of Canaan for an everlasting possession. This is my covenant, and you shall proclaim the circumcision of every male among you. You shall give your wife Sarai a new name, Sarah, and I will give you a son by her and he shall be called Isaac." So, Abraham circumcised all males, whether born or bought into his household.

In the meantime, the Lord instructed Lot, who lived in Sodom, to leave the city with his wife and two daughters as he was about to destroy Sodom and Gomorrah with rains of brimstone and fire because of the grievous sins of the people. As they leave, Lot's wife becomes a pillar of salt because she looked back. Lot dwells in the mountains with his two daughters who were without a man except for their father. They made him drink wine and laid with him. One bore a son, Moab, who became the father of the Moabites, and the other bore Ben-ammi, who became the father of the Ammonites.

Then Abraham journeyed to the land of King Abimelech where he again proclaimed Sarah to be his sister again for self- protection. The king took Sarah, but upon learning that she was Abraham's wife, the king asked Abraham to swear by God that he would not again deal falsely with him nor with his offspring. Abraham then gave the King seven sheep and oxen. To maintain his integrity, Abimelech returned Sarah to her husband and sent them to dwell wherever they pleased.

Sarah then conceived and bore Abraham a son, Isaac. Isaac matured and Sarah asked that the son of her servant, Hagar, born to Abraham, to be cast out since Ishmael would not be heir. This grieved Abraham because Ishmael was his son. But a vision of God told Abraham to not grieve because Ishmael will be father to a nation, so Hagar and Ishmael left the household.

After these things, God, testing Abraham's faith, told him to take his son to the land of Moriah and sacrifice him there on the mountain. So, Abraham rose in the morning and took his son Isaac. He cut the wood and took it to where God told him to sacrifice Isaac as a burnt offering. He bound and laid Isaac on the wood and took in his hand the fire and the knife. But the Lord intervened to protect and bless Isaac. Abraham saw a ram caught in a thicket, so instead he offered the ram as the sacrifice to the Lord.

*

The story of Abraham is a story of a long series of crises beginning with being told by the Lord that he had to leave the land of his father and move to the land of the Canaanites, where he would become the father of a great nation. Once in Canaan, there was a severe famine, so Abram and Sarai went on to Egypt. Because of his wife's beauty, he feared for his life. The Pharaoh took her, but then blamed her for a plague that struck the land so sent them back to Canaan where he prospered.

The Lord again assured him that after 400 years of servitude to the Canaanites this land would become the land of his progeny, and the Lord changed his name from Abram to Abraham and Sarai to Sarah. Though unable to conceive, Lord assured Sarah she would bear her husband a son to be named Isaac. Finally, when Abraham was 99 years old, she gave him a son, but the biggest crisis occurred when the Lord told him he had to sacrifice his son. When Abraham was about to make the sacrifice, because of his obedience, the Lord stopped him.

Listening to the Story of Abraham

To journey with the Story of Abraham, the group of five stood in the Feathered Serpent Posture (Fig. 3.5), an initiation or death-rebirth posture.

Donna

During the time of following my breath to quiet the mind, I see the underbelly of Quetzalcoatl, the Feathered Serpent. The feathers are varying shades of white and cream, and vibrant blues of azure and teal. The creature, flying overhead in my perspective, is close enough for me to feel the warmth and lush texture of the feathered underbelly, almost as if I am being carried beneath. We are flying over the Northern Hemisphere, crossing central North America from east to west. Suddenly we make a sharp turn counterclockwise at the Grand Canyon and we fly south, gaining energy while passing over the pyramids and sacred sites on my journey into Central and South America. My body is increasingly infused with energy coming up from my feet and vibrating up to above my right eye in the general location of my pineal gland. My sinuses and the cavities in my cranium fill with liquid energy, a substance somewhere between water/oil and fire. This liquid softens my skull and creates larger and wider sinus cavities. The shape of my head changes as my eye sockets widen, and the bone matrix becomes thinner, lighter, and more hollow. The bones through my torso are thin and elongate, with my head enlarging and my lower body diminishing from the waist down.

About half-way through holding the posture, a bright flash of electric blue-green energy passes up from the earth into my body, entering through the soles of my feet. At this point my lower body seems superfluous, and the posture ends with me looking down at stick-thin, bright yellow bird legs and feet.

Returning to Her Ka Body

As with Donna's Adam and Eve journey, again she turns south at the Grand Canyon to find her spirit body. On this Abrahamic journey, she flies under the belly of Quetzalcoatl, the feathered serpent who crawls on the Earth but gains the feathers to fly in the heavens. She is the Aztec deity of life, light, and wisdom, lord of the day and the winds. In carrying Donna into the heavens, she is a transformative deity, carrying her from her root chakra up into the spirit world like the serpents of the Kundalini.

The energy Donna gains as she passes over the sacred pyramids of Central and South America is a vibrant blue energy that passes up through her feet and through her lower chakra to her throat chakra. The blue energy of her throat chakra infuses her cranial sinus cavities with a liquid energy somewhere between water/oil and fire. Her body transforms with this energy, expanding her head and eye sockets while her lower body from the waist down atrophies to chicken legs, bringing alive her spiritual Ka Body or Spirit Body.

Abraham's life journey is a journey of transformation, bringing him to become the father of a great nation, but again Donna's transformation takes her beyond her physical body and into the spirit world, a harbinger of the future, of Joseph's journey into the spiritual world of dreams, taking her into the world of the beauty of her Goddess-Consciousness, leaving behind the patriarchal world of the struggle between good and evil, between us vs. them. Abraham's journey to become the father of a great nation is a journey that remains in the patriarchal, physical world.

Lauren

While standing in the Feathered Serpent Posture, I am onstage, a ballet dancer, dancing my staccato dance to the beat of the drum, part African and part Native American. I'm on pointe shoes, moving up and down with the beat, high on my toes and then down on my heels, knees bent, back slumped, head down to my feet. I am then back up! Like a marionette. I'm bending my rigid limbs at sharp angles. I am dancing with a snake as my partner. He is huge, with a black raccoon-like mask around his eyes. And he has enormous paws, like a dragon or a dinosaur. I am not sure, but there are several of them. I am dancing around a campfire and the serpents surround me. Though the situation appears ominous, I am not afraid. I know how to control them. I take a burning ember from the fire in my hand. As I take it closer to each creature, he backs away. I continue dancing, more tribal than balletic.

Then I am the Buddha, sitting by the fire in meditation. All that has occurred has happened in the imaginal realm, my imagination. I realize I wasn't controlling the serpents with my knowledge of their fear of fire, but with my own thoughts. The serpents represent my desires and are frightened when I don't reveal my desires, coming closer to terrorize me, but I can remove my attention from them and they back away.

Now I am again the dancer, and sitting across from me is the Buddha. I try to meditate with him but can't stand the stillness. Movement is my meditation. I get up and dance, inviting the creatures to dance. A baby then shows up. How cute! I get closer to the creatures to connect with their sweet raccoon faces. One comes very close. I see its split tongue, its fangs, its cold, green eyes, and scaly skin. Yikes! No, thank you. With my thoughts, I send it back. My thoughts send everything back. I'm neither the dancer nor the Buddha. I consciously retreat from the scene. I'm still watching, as if I'm shining a spotlight on the stage, moving further and further back until I am way out in space, in the middle of the solar system. I feel very far removed. I hang out for a while, but this really isn't fun. I want to come back and connect, so I do. Now, as a man, I do a Greek or Jewish line dance. My body feels strong and alive. I feel passionate and invincible. But I want to play, to become a clown or court jester, so I do a forward roll. I then get up, back to being the man.

Dancing with the Serpent

Like Donna's experience of returning to her Adam and Eve experience of journeying south into Central and South America, Lauren also returns to the motif of her Adam and Eve journey of dancing with the snake. This time the snake, more like a dragon, possibly the feathered serpent but without the feathers, exists in the lower world of the Root Chakra.

Lauren's preference for entering the world of the spirits is through dance, movement that feels more alive. Meditation, as with Buddha, does not work for her. In dancing on stage, she is dancing like a marionette, bending her limbs at right angles. Her dance partner is again a huge reptile with a raccoon like mask and huge paws. Though the situation appears ominous, she is not afraid, because she knows how to control him with a burning ember of fire. But she then realizes that her control is not from the ember but with her thoughts. If she removes her attention from the serpents, they back away. Paying attention to them, they can become terrorizing.

In moving close to a baby serpent, seeing its split tongue, fangs, and scaly skin frightens her such that she moves back, way out into space where she finds little fun, so she returns and feels strong, alive, and invincible in her ability to control the situation.

How does her experience of feeling strength, knowing she has control over potential terrorizing crises, fit with the story of Abraham? Abraham's strength is listening to the Lord, listening in his world of dreams and visions. He does not have control over what he visions like Lauren, thus, Lauren goes beyond his world, again a harbinger of going into the dreamworld of Joseph, the world of understanding the dreams brought to him. Again, as with Donna, she goes beyond the patriarchal story of Abraham, taking her into her inner matriarchal world of the Mother Goddess, the Goddess-Consciousness within her.

Henning

I soar up high above the barren lands of Canaan as Noah's Dove, while standing in the flying Feathered Serpent Posture. I am taking a survey, an inventory of the land promised Abram. There is not much to note there. It doesn't seem like much of a reward for the pain of having had to leave home and everything that was familiar.

I become the observer of Abraham on the morning when he is to sacrifice his son, Isaac. Abraham, tormented since receiving the order from God, throws up after a night of crying fits. "Why, why, why?!" It goes round and round in his head. But he finds the answer: There is no 'Why.' There is only the Grand Plan, and this is part of it. I will/must follow it.

He hikes up a hill with his son, whose form switches back and forth throughout the scene from that of a baby to that of a 12-year-old. "Why, father?" Abraham answers in tears, "Have faith, son." He raises a knife, held in both hands over his son's head, ready to thrust it into Isaac's chest. He would gladly kill himself instead, but he knows he can't do that, as it is not the way. Abraham is shaky, worn, and somewhat broken after he sacrificed the ram. His faith is strong, but his body and mind are infinitely tired.

Visions of Abraham's Crises

Henning, in his travels with Abraham, soars high over the Earth not as the Feathered Serpent but as Noah's Dove, observing the Earth below him, responding to two of Abraham's crises. First, the barren-desolate land of the Canaanites that Abraham is about to enter as an immigrant, land that is suffering a famine. The second and the last crisis he observes is when Abraham is about to sacrifice his young son Isaac, and the excruciating pain he is feeling, yet his obedience to the words he experiences coming from the Lord gives him the needed reprieve. In response, exhausted, he sacrifices a ram. Entering the new age, the world of the Mother Goddess takes sacrifice, leaving behind the feeling of power and control of patriarchy, as he finds the beauty of the matriarchal world of the Mother Goddess.

Lonnie

> Using the Feathered Serpent Posture, as Abraham, larger than life, I stand on the mountain top and see the twinkling lights of the village below with people milling about. I focus and see Sarah, not my wife, but my niece with her husband David and a little baby in her arms. It pleases me. It's cold on top of the mountain and standing in the posture is very tiring. I think to myself, "I've done this long enough," and I descend the mountain. As I do, I notice the villagers are coming up to meet me. We all embrace, and I am happy to see the village come together.

Abraham, the Father of a Future Great Nation

In ecstatic trance, I journey with Lonnie as he journeys with Abraham. Abraham, in his Ka Body, is standing larger than life on a mountain top, observing future descendants of his great nation. As he goes down to mingle with them, they are on their way up to honor him. Again, Lonnie's experience expresses positive feelings of love of the Mother Goddess and avoids the pain of other aspects of the patriarchal Abraham story.

Nick

From the time of my review of Matthew Wood's book, on my journey with Abraham, I am standing over, straddling, a fast-moving stream of water and in this posture of the Feathered Serpent I cannot lift my leg back over the stream to the other side to extract myself from this situation. The water is ice cold and I do not want to go in, but I eventually realize that the only thing I can do is to get wet. The stream is deep enough so I am not sure that I will not be washed down, or I will fall off balance into the water, but I let go of my fear and put one foot in the water. It finds the bottom, but I must put my other foot in too for balance. I can then turn and climb out to safety.

A Sacrifice to Resolve a Crisis

For Abraham to resolve the crisis of having to sacrifice his son, he must sacrifice something such as the Ram, just as I had to sacrifice getting both legs wet to get across the stream. What am I sacrificing on my journey into the new world of the Mother Goddess? I sacrifice my patriarchal power and control that feels important to me as a man in following my vision of God, but once I am free of it, the love and beauty of the world of matriarchy is clearly preferred.

> In the experience with the ecstatic trance group, I first see a coyote coming to me, laughing at me, challenging me, but about what? Coyote experiences of the past come to me, beginning with the bear, honeybee, and coyote, challenging me on why I was unwilling to share the honey with the bear.
>
> I then become Abraham ready to sacrifice Isaac and the coyote again is laughing at me in my determination to do something so crazy, because I was told to do it in a vision of God. I then look to our Great Earth Mother and ask what would she do? She would be nurturing. She would do nothing to test my faith or challenge me, but then I realized that in her love she sent me Coyote to challenge me in all my rigid beliefs.

The Laughing Coyote

As Abraham, the coyote is laughing at me in my crazy determination to sacrifice my son. We need to trust nature and our nurturing Great Earth Mother, who does not test our faith. The God of

Abraham is a punishing God, which makes no sense in creating a world of nurturing love.

Ecstatic Revelation of Abraham

Except for the experience of Henning's and my first experience, the other four experiences took our experiences beyond the story of Abraham. Donna and Lauren's experiences were harbingers of Joseph in his ability to see beyond the physical to the spiritual, as offered by his ability to understand the meanings of dreams. Lonnie's Ka experience took him into the future to see the future of his descendants in the new Great Nation, and my experience with the group was again to find the nurturing love of our Great Earth Mother as opposed to the punishing nature of the patriarchal God of Abraham.

Henning's experience was a vision of two of the crises of Abraham: of arriving in the famine-stricken land of the Canaanites and of the sacrifice of his son, Isaac. My first experience was of the need to make a sacrifice to resolve a crisis.

CHAPTER 8

Isaac

The Story of Isaac

Recalling the birth of Isaac, as we heard in the story of Abraham, his mother Sarah was barren, though the Lord had promised Abraham offspring. When Abraham was 99, she became pregnant and had Isaac. But the Lord continued to test/tempt Abraham, telling him to sacrifice Isaac. When Abraham was about to kill Isaac on the altar, the Lord intervened to stop him. Then Abraham saw a ram caught in a nearby thicket and sacrificed it instead.

After Sarah's death, Abraham took another wife, Keturah, with whom he had six more children before his death at the age of 175 years of age, but he gave all he had to Isaac. When Isaac was of age, Abraham sent his oldest household servant out to find him a wife, but not a Canaanite woman. The servant questioned if the woman would return with him, and Abraham answered that an angel of the Lord would come down and tell her and her family that she should go. The servant departed with 10 camels. When seeking water for himself and the camels, he knew to trust the woman who would come out for water. Rebekah was the one, the granddaughter of Abraham's brother. Being blessed by the Lord in this way, she returned with the servant to Isaac.

Isaac, at 40 years of age, prayed to the Lord because Rebekah was barren. The Lord granted his prayer, and she conceived. The twins within her womb struggled together. She asked the Lord about this struggle, and the Lord told her: "Two divided nations are in your womb. The older shall be stronger than the younger, but the older shall serve the younger." The first born, named Esau, came out with his body like a hairy cloak. His brother, named Jacob, followed with his hand hanging on to Esau's heel. Though Isaac favored Esau, Rebekah favored Jacob.

There was a famine in the land and the Lord told Isaac to go dwell in the land that he shall show him. The Lord will be with him, bless him, and give him and his offspring all these lands. So, Isaac settled in the land shown him, but when the men of the place asked him about his wife he said, "She is my sister," for he feared to say, "My wife," thinking the men would kill him because of Rebekah's beauty. When the king discovered this, he warned all the people, "Whoever touches this man I shall put to death."

Isaac sowed and reaped in the land and became rich. With the Lord's blessing, he possessed flocks and herds and many servants. But, because of the envy of the people since he was much mightier than the others, the King told him to leave.

Isaac settled in the Valley of Gerar and dug wells for water where Abraham's wells had been. The Philistines had filled in the wells after Abraham's death. But the herdsmen quarreled over the water, so Isaac dug another well and again they quarreled over it. So, he dug a third well and called it Rehoboth, saying the Lord has made room for us and we shall be fruitful.

The Lord appeared in a vision and said: "Fear not I'm the God of Abraham. I am with you and bless you." So there Isaac built an altar. The king, seeing that Isaac was blessed, came, and sought a covenant with him to do no harm, so they held a feast and there was peace.

Esau, the older son, made life bitter for Isaac and Rebekah. Isaac was going blind and called Esau to him, telling him to go hunt game so that he could eat and that he would bless Esau. Rebekah, hearing this deceived Isaac by telling Jacob to fetch two goats from the flock, and then she dressed him as Esau. Jacob went to Isaac and said I'm Esau, so eat and bless me, and he received Isaac's blessing. When Isaac discovered this deception, he told Esau, by your sword you shall live and serve your brother, but when restless, you shall break his neck. When Rebekah heard the words from Esau, she told

Jacob of his brother's plan to kill him. She told him that he should arise and flee to her brother Laban, and when Esau turns away from his anger, she will send for him. Rebekah feared though that Jacob would take a Canaanite woman to marry, and Isaac told him not to do so. But Esau displeased his father by taking a Canaanite woman for his wife.

We journey with Isaac using the Calling the Spirits Posture (Fig. 3.6).

Donna

Upon standing and assuming the posture of Calling the Spirits, my body becomes hot. Heat radiates from the ground into the soles of my feet and up my legs. Swaying while in trance, a smoky fire appears before me. Beings, adorned in feathers and wearing animal skins, are dancing around it. As they dance, there is an air of the macabre. It is night, and I stand outside this inner circle of shamans. The charged atmosphere feels exciting and mischievous, but not for me. I am the observer and remain neutral.

Somehow, perhaps by my swaying, I am identified and removed from the group. The shamans wrap my body in a cloth and place me in a shallow hole, which is covered with long, leafy branches.

I lie there face up for three days and three nights. The sky changes rapidly from day to night as I watch in some type of altered state, immobile and outside of time.

Next, I emerge, alone, as a thin young man. Wearing only a loincloth. I wander the desert as a mystic nomad. As I transverse the arid landscape, I want nothing and need nothing. At one point, I arrive at a village. Someone brings me a prayer rug to sit on, which I place under a date tree where I meditate. There are others like me there, and we sit with our backs against a low stone wall. Not allowed inside the village perimeters, people come out to be blessed by us.

The journey continues with no clear destination. At one point a bird of prey appears, perhaps a vulture, as tall if not taller than me, and pecks out my spleen. There is no pain or attack, it is a healing or a cleansing ritual, and the animal feels like an ally.

My nomadic desert meanderings continue and as the drumming slows a purple/green light descends from the sky. I walk into the light and disappear.

Donna's Spiritual Powers

Donna found herself part of a group of shamans, and when the shaman discovered her as an outsider, they buried her, and she remained there while in trance and outside of time for three days and three nights. She emerged from this ritual as a nomadic wandering mystic who the people seek. In her wandering, a vulture pecked out her spleen, a healing and cleansing ritual. She then disappears in a purple/green light, the light of her crown chakra descending from the sky, again connecting her to her Ka or Spiritual Body, her Goddess-Consciousness.

How does Donna's experience fit with the story of Isaac? Isaac, in prayer, was effective in communing with the Lord, showing his shamanic or mystical powers. When deceived, he accepted the deception as a reminder of his wife's much earlier vision of the Lord saying that Esau shall serve Jacob, his younger brother. This forgiving acceptance is a personal cleansing for his allegiance to Esau. Yet, Donna remains a step ahead of Isaac in her shamanic/spiritual powers, as seen when people come to her seeking her spiritual wisdom. Her connection to her Ka or Spiritual Body, her Goddess-Consciousness, is again a harbinger of the powers of Joseph and reflects her journey into the new world of the Mother Goddess.

Lauren

In Calling the Spirits, I am looking down at a tiny snail. I see its two little antennae. It is white, gooey, and ugly. I become the snail and know the snail is also Isaac. He is calling on God for protection from being sacrificed, and the shell is the gift he has received.

Then a goofy, cartoon-like ghost appears. It seems to have emerged from the snail. It's not scary; is it God? It doesn't really do anything but just hangs out being a ghost that's vaguely attached to the snail's shell. The ghost then retreats and becomes part of the shell again.

I guess this is a metaphor. The spirit that Isaac is calling on is really part of him; the answers are from within him. The safety he finds in the shell comes from within him.

I feel the drumming and want to move. I move my physical body within the meditation. Suddenly, there are many, many snails out front of our house making a wide circle around the fire pit. The snails leave their shells to dance, but they're too frightened to go far from the shells. So, each snail dances alone around his own shell. The pearly shells are beautiful, but the snails seem small and lonely, each dancing alone.

The sun comes out and nearly all the snails dry up and die, leaving only a few.

Isaac is despondent over his son's deception, and more so over Rebekah's betrayal.

Incidentally, I don't feel very connected with the Isaac story. I don't care about standing postures and didn't feel well during this one. All I wanted to do was to sit down. This trance time seemed very long and, uncharacteristically, I just wanted to get it over with.

The Protective Shells of the Snail/Isaac

Lauren becomes a gooey and ugly snail, knowing that the snail is Isaac. The vision of a ghost rising from the snail represents Isaac's protection from being sacrificed. Though the Holy Ghost or Spirit initially called to Abraham to sacrifice Isaac, he also protects Isaac in the end, a spirit that Lauren recognizes as being part of Isaac, like her Goddess-Consciousness is part of Lauren.

Leaving their protecting Spirits, the snails leave their shells
and dance alone close to their beautiful shells. But when the sun
comes out many die, a death of Isaac's corrupt preference for Esau
when earlier at the time of their birth, the Holy Spirit told his wife,
Rebekah, that Jacob was to be a leader in the coming Great Nation
with Esau serving him.

Lauren did not identify with this story as the need for protection. She was again ahead of Isaac in understanding and being part
of the world of the spirits, her Goddess-Consciousness, as seen in
the future story of Joseph.

Henning

I struggle with the dishonesty in the betrayal of Esau by
Jacob scene where Rebekah dresses her son Jacob in furs
to pretend that he was Esau to receive his father Isaac's
blessing and inheritance. According to some sources, Esau
had previously bequeathed his heirloom to his brother for
a bowl of soup, so the whole charade is a process of the
rightful transfer of the inheritance. However, deception is
not something I can easily witness. So, I call myself to the
posture of Calling the Spirits. As I lift my chin higher, more
breath enters my body through my throat, the 5th chakra,
as we are in the 5th of 7 stories of Genesis. The throat is the
gateway of truth and breath, which vividly opens the gateway to the spirit of life at this moment. I play with the micro-
cosmic orbit; what goes around my energetic body, up my
back and over my head, then down the front of my torso, is
a breath that carries both the sun and the moon on opposite
sides of the orbit. I inhale sunlight from all pores and parts
of my body and aura, and radiate out ALL FREQUENCIES
of the visible, audible, and heat spectra.

Experiencing the Energy of the Spirit World
Henning struggles with the dishonesty of Rebekah and Jacob in

deceiving Isaac, so going into trance with the Calling the Spirits Posture that carries him to his fifth chakra, the throat chakra that is the gateway of truth and breath, the gateway for the fifth story of Genesis. He feels the energy of his spirit body flowing up over his head and back down the front of his torso, carrying both the sun and the moon on opposite sides of this orbit. In inhaling the sunlight, all pores and parts of his body radiate in his aura all frequencies of the visible, audible and heat spectra. The spiritual energy of his Ka/Spirit Body carries him into the new world of his Goddess-Consciousness beyond these stories that remain in the patriarchal physical world.

Lonnie

In standing in the Calling the Spirits Posture, I step out on my front porch. It is dark. There is a full moon that is setting. Having no sense of the time, I look to see what time it is but don't have my watch or phone and can't get back into the house. I don't know the time, which causes me to feel anxious.

The light increases, and I see my dog, Roxy, running up to me. She is very young and energetic. I'm confused. What is happening to the time? With the increase in light, I can make out two figures. It should be my two horses, but they appear to be two brothers quarreling. I look again to see the time, but I can't. It is dark again. My open mouth is the entrance to a dark tunnel going down my throat. I don't know how far it goes, but it feels like the door to a different world. I want to go down, but it feels cold and damp. I'm afraid I might find this new world filled with water. I'm scared.

Facing His Anxieties and Fears of the World of the Spirits
Lonnie, having no sense of time and feeling confused suggests that he is experiencing deep trance. His disassociation from time

is causing him anxiety, likely due to what he might discover in the darkness of his trance. Such anxiety is not uncommon and the reason that I usually offer an ego strengthening exercise before entering trance. The trauma that is frequently uncovered in trance is the source of such anxiety, and in this case, the conflict and quarrel between the two brothers, Jacob and Esau, is likely the trauma. When he sees in the shadows of the two brothers quarreling, his anxiety rises, and he again seeks to find out the time and it again becomes dark. Lonnie's nature is to avoid conflict and quarrels.

He then realizes that his open mouth is an entrance to a dark tunnel going down his throat, the entryway to honesty, a fearful, cold, and damp tunnel. In going down the tunnel to his root chakra, he would face these insecurities and fears, the conflict between the two brothers. When openly faced, he would find strength and protection, but it is something he avoids in the positive way he faces life that brings others to him in love. Again, Lonnie avoids facing conflict by looking to the positive of the love of the Mother Goddess, his Goddess-Consciousness.

Nick

At the time of reviewing Matthew Wood's book, I used the Calling the Spirits Posture to journey with Isaac. I stand with my mouth open, waiting for the spirits. I stop to think in which direction am I facing and realize it is to the East. I am confident that the spirits of the East will come to me, and sure enough I see the sun rising over the hills and feel the warmth of the new day. It's going to be a warm spring day. I go to our garden and dig a shallow trench along one bed, and lay a row of lettuce seed, cover it over and pat it down, looking forward to having some spring lettuce. I feel the spirits telling me it is not too early to plant the seed though we still could have another frost before it comes up. As I sit next to the newly planted row, feeling the warmth of the sun, I see a rabbit hopping across the lawn and know that it too would like the lettuce, so I cover the row with a light fabric to protect it, though I know it is not much of a barrier for a rabbit. The spirits of the East are giving me instructions for what I must do.

Listening to the Spirits

In my gardening, I call upon and listen to the spirits to make gardening decisions. What does this have to do with Isaac? Throughout the story of Isaac, he listens to the spirits. Isaac's father, Abraham, did not sacrifice him when he was told by the Holy Spirit not to. When Rebekah did not become pregnant, Isaac brought the problem to the Holy Spirit, and he received the wanted answer. Rebekah received an answer when she felt the twins inside of her quarreling. When Isaac was going blind and deceived in giving his blessing to Jacob instead of Esau, again the words of the Spirit came to him that Esau was to serve Jacob, the younger brother. The story of Isaac was of calling to and listening to the spirit as was my experience of listening to the spirits for making garden decisions, listening to the Mother Goddess, my Goddess-Consciousness.

In my Isaac experience with the group, I survey or review the story of Isaac. I become Isaac and my dad, Abraham, takes me up on the mountain and instructs me to lie on an altar he built. He then pulls out his knife and holds it above me. I call out "Why, why, why?" He was a loving father I trusted. I can see tears in his eyes as I continue to call out, "Why?" He then looks up, gasps and puts down his knife and reaches down to me, pulling me up to hug. I know he was hearing or seeing something, but I do not know what. He then beckons to me to follow him up to the ram that was stuck in a thorn bush, and he cuts the artery on his neck as we cut away the bush from him and bring him down to the altar where dad raises his arms to the heavens, still crying, but with a smile and calling out "Thank you, Thank you."

After Abraham dies, there is a famine on the land, and

I, as Isaac, know I need to leave where I had been living and return to where I lived with my father Abraham, knowing that there was good water there, but when I get there, all the wells are all filled in. I instructed my servants/herders to dig out the wells, but as they do, they quarrel among themselves over which wells to use, and which has better water. They then dig another well for me and Rebekah and stop quarreling, because I am with them. I remember Abraham telling me that the Lord had given him and his descendants this land so it would go to me. I see the truth in this belief because it is now my land, and we prosper upon it.

But concerned that I have no descendants, that Rebekah is barren, I pray to the Lord and have a dream that she will become pregnant, which she does. This is the one time I call out to the Lord, and he answers me, again validating the beliefs of my father. Rebekah knows she has twins because she can feel them fighting within her and she prays, asking why. She receives the answer that the younger of the two would serve the older, something that was against the expectations of the time. The first born, Esau, is hairy and strong, and will be a hunter. The second, Jacob, comes out hanging onto the foot of Esau. Esau's strength helps in pulling Jacob out of the womb. Isaac loves Esau most, while Rebekah made up for this favoritism by showing her love for Jacob.

When Isaac is old and blind, he knows he is about to die and it is time for him to bless his oldest son, Esau, so sends him out on a hunt to bring home some animal that they can feast on. Rebekah, hearing this, calls Jacob to her, dresses him in Esau's clothing, and places animal hides over his arms such that when he goes to his father, his father will think it is Esau. Abraham then blesses him, Jacob, thinking it is the older brother. When Esau returns, his father realizes his mistake, knowing that what he did makes Esau a servant to Jacob as the Lord had told Rebekah at the time of their birth. Again, Isaac finds validation for the words of the Lord, again a validating experience that Rebekah's dream and vision was reliable, valid, and real.

Validation of the Words Coming from the Spirit.
The psychologist Peter Ralston's[1] major thesis is that a belief can easily lead a person astray unless validated by experience. Isaac took the beliefs taught him by his father and validated them through experience.

Each event in the story of Isaac was a validation of the words of the Spirit. Abraham did not sacrifice Isaac when he listened to the spirit. Isaac prospers on the land that was promised him by the Holy Spirit. Isaac prayed to the Spirit that Rebekah would become pregnant, and she did. Rebekah prayed about the twins quarreling within her womb, and she received the answer that the older would serve the younger, which was validated as the story progressed and deceptively Jacob received Isaac's blessing instead of Esau, again validating the voice of the spirit, the voice coming from his Goddess-Consciousness.

Ecstatic Revelation of Isaac

Each of the five experiences concerned listening to the spirits, whether for Donna to gain spiritual power, Lauren to gain protection, Henning to find greater energy, Lonnie to find strength in facing anxiety and fear, or Nick to validate the words of the spirit. Listening to the spirits, the voice of our Goddess-Consciousness, became alive and was most important to each person of the group, as well as to Isaac and Rebekah.

CHAPTER 9

Jacob

The Story of Jacob

Rebekah when pregnant felt the twins within her struggling. With this struggle, she received a vision that though Esau was the oldest, he would serve his younger brother, Jacob. After their birth, once Jacob was cooking stew when Esau came in from the field exhausted and asked for some stew. Jacob said to him, "Sell me your birthright." Esau said, "I am about to die, so what use is my birthright," so he sold his birthright to Jacob.

The older brother, Esau, made life bitter for Isaac, their father, and Rebekah, their mother. When Isaac was going blind, he called Esau to him to bless him. Rebekah, hearing this, prepared Jacob to deceive his father to receive the blessing. So, Isaac blessed Jacob by mistake, "May God give you of the dew of heaven, the fatness of the Earth and plants of grain and wine. Let the people serve you."

Then Esau came to Isaac, trembling in violence. Isaac told him, "I have made Jacob lord over you," and Esau wept. Isaac suggested to Esau that when restless, he should break his brother's neck. These words Esau told Rebekah, so she told Jacob of his brother's plan to kill him, and that he should arise and flee to her brother, Laban.

As Jacob journeyed to his uncle's, and when the sun set, he laid down to sleep and had a dream: "Behold a ladder to heaven with Angels of God ascending and descending it. An Angel said, 'With God's blessing, this land I give you and your offspring. Your offspring shall be like the dust of the earth, and you shall spread abroad to the west and to the east and to the north and to the south.' Jacob woke and said, 'Surely the Lord is in this place, and I did not know it.' And he made a vow to God: 'I shall return to my father's house in peace, the Lord shall be my God, and I will give a full tenth of what I make to him.'"

Jacob then came to a well, and three flocks of sheep were lying beside it to be watered. Rachel, the daughter of Laban, came with the sheep. Jacob, upon seeing Rachel went to Laban and told him he will serve him for seven years to marry Rachel. The seven years seemed like a few days because of his love for Rachel. But at the end of the seven years Laban brought the older sister Leah to him, saying that the older must marry before the younger. So, Jacob was to have two wives, but he loved Rachel more.

The Lord opened the womb of the less favored, leaving Rachel barren. Leah conceived a son Reuben, then conceived again and had Simeon and then again giving him Levi, and then Judah.

Rachel envied Leah and told Jacob, "Give me children or I shall die." Then Rachel gave him one of her servants so that she may give birth on her behalf. The servant conceived a son and Rachel said that God has heard her voice and gave her a son who she called Dan, and a second son of the servant she called Naphtali. But Leah who was now barren, seeing this, gave Jacob one of her servants who gave him another son who she named Gad, and then a second son, Asher.

Reuben found mandrakes in the field and brought them to his mother Leah. Rachel, seeing this asked Leah for some mandrakes. (Wow! It gets more and more complex). Leah told Rachel that she has taken her husband and now she wants her son's mandrakes. In response, Rachel offered Leah Jacob for the night, and she conceived a fifth son, Issachar, and a sixth named Zebulun, and then a daughter, Dinah.

God, remembering Rachel, then opens her womb, and Rachel conceives, "saying God has taken away my reproach." Thus, Joseph was born. With this, Jacob tells Laban that it is time for him to return to his own home and country. Laban prospered, recognizing that the Lord had blessed him because of Jacob. Thus, Laban offered Jacob wages for the work he had done before he returns home. Jacob requested to take from Laban's herd the speckled and spotted sheep, the black lambs, and the speckled and spotted goats as his wages. But Laban removes the male goats that were spotted and striped and the female goats that were speckled and spotted and every black lamb, giving them to his son, and gave the son a three-day head-start between himself and Jacob.

But Jacob took fresh sticks of poplar and almond, peeled white streaks in them, exposing the white of the sticks. He set the sticks in front of watering troughs where the flocks came to drink and breed, so the flock brought forth striped, speckled, and spotted lambs. Jacob separates the lambs and set the flock to face the striped and all the black in the flock of Laban. He puts the sticks in the watering troughs so that they would breed among the sticks, producing feeble offspring. Thus, Laban's flock is feeble and Jacob's strong.

Seeing that Laban no longer regards Jacob with favor, the Lord said to Jacob, "Return to the Land of your father and I will be with you." So, he calls Rachel and Leah into the field, tells them that their father has cheated him and that the Lord told him to arise and go to the land of his kindred. Jacob sees in a dream Angels of God. "Here I am. Lift your eyes and see, all the goats that mate with the flock are striped, spotted, and mottled, for I have seen all that Laban has done to you." Rachel and Leah noted all the wealth that God had taken from their father belonged to them, so they went with Jacob. Jacob sent his sons and wives on camels and drove away with all the livestock that he had gained and left to return to his father, Isaac. Laban was away shearing his sheep and Rachel stole her father's household gods. They then left, crossing the Euphrates, and set out towards the hill country of Gilead.

On the third day, Laban discovered Jacob had fled and took out after him into the hill country. But the God of Isaac came to Laban in a dream and told him, "Be careful not to say anything good or bad to Jacob." Laban pursued Jacob and caught up with him. Each accused the other of trickery. Laban complained Jacob took his daughters, their children without saying goodbye, and his household gods. Jacob knew nothing about Laban's household gods, so Laban went in search of the gods and when he searched in Rachel's tent, she was sitting on the camel saddle bag that held them, saying that she could not stand because she was again with child. So, Laban left.

Jacob, in anger accused Laban for not treating him fairly after he had worked for Laban for 20 years, 14 years for the hands of his daughters and 6 years for his share of Laban's flock. Laban said, all you see is mine, but let's make a covenant. So Jacob made a stone pillar, and they agreed that when they were out of each other's sight Jacob would not pass by the stones to do Laban harm and Laban would not pass by the stones to harm Jacob. So they swore before their Gods, the God of Abraham and the God of Nahor. The next morning, they arose, and Laban kissed his daughters and grandchildren goodbye. They went in opposite directions, with Jacob returning to the home of Isaac.

At the bank of the Jordan River, Jacob sent a messenger ahead to tell Esau that he was returning with his wealth and family. The messenger returned to Jacob, telling him that Esau was coming to meet him with 400 men, a message that frightened Jacob. He prayed to God who assured him of Esau's acceptance in his return home. But Jacob divided his camp in two, with his staff preparing to cross the Jordan, taking a present of two hundred female goats, twenty male goats, two hundred ewes and twenty rams, thirty milking camels and their calves, forty cows and ten bulls, twenty female donkeys and ten male donkeys. He sent them ahead with his servants to tell Esau that they are a gift to him.

Jacob then sent his wives and all that was his across the river, and he was alone. A man (an angel of the Lord) came to him, and they wrestled until daybreak, and when the angel did not prevail, he touched Jacob's hip and put it out of joint as they continued to wrestle, but Jacob would not let go of the man until the angel blessed him. The man then told Jacob that he was no longer to be called Jacob, but Israel, for he has striven with God and with men and has prevailed. To this day the people of Israel do not eat the sinew of the thigh that is on the hip socket because the angel of the Lord touched it.

When Jacob looked up, he saw Esau coming with his 400 men. He put the servants in front of Leah and her sons, with Rachel and Joseph at the back and went to meet Esau, bowing to the ground seven times before Esau. Esau ran to him and embraced him and fell on his neck and kissed him. As they greeted and Esau learned of Jacob's wives and children, Esau said that he had enough and did not want the gifts offered him by Jacob, but Jacob insisted. Esau said, "Let us journey on our way and I will lead you." So, Esau and Jacob journey each to their own land, with Jacob buying a piece of land for a hundred pieces of money.

Dinah, Jacob's one daughter, goes out to see the women of the land when the prince of the land sees her, seizes her, and lays with her, humiliating her. The father of the prince comes to Jacob, wanting Dinah for his son's wife, but Jacob and his sons are indignant and angry. The King then offers land to Jacob to dwell and trade on, and he offers his daughters to Jacob. But Dinah's brothers say that the prince has defiled her, and they cannot give their sister to one who is uncircumcised. The prince eagerly agrees to be circumcised, and the King tells his people that all men need to be circumcised, so they were. But on the third day Simeon and Levi, Dinah's brothers, go against the city with their swords and kill all the males, including the prince, take Dinah out of the house along with all the wealth of the city. What Simeon and Levi did bring trouble to Jacob, knowing that the people of the king will seek to destroy his household.

God then said to Jacob, "Arise and go up to Bethel and dwell there." So, Jacob prepares his household to move and makes an altar to the God who answered him on the day of his distress. Jacob asks that all with him give him all the foreign gods and earrings that they have, and he hides them under a tree. So, they journey and a terror from God falls upon the cities, protecting Jacob on his journey. Upon arriving, God appears again and blesses him, and tells him his name shall be Israel.

Rachel goes into hard labor during which she dies, but she has a son that Jacob calls Benjamin. So, Jacob buries Rachel in what is now Bethlehem. Jacob then comes to his father Isaac now 180 years of age. Isaac breaths his last and his sons Esau and Jacob bury him. Jacob then lives in the land of his father.

*

To journey with the story of Jacob, we used the Jama Coaque Metamorphosis Posture (Fig. 3.7).

Donna

At some point, midway through the smudging, I see an infinity sign behind my closed eyelids. This symbol, which has appeared this way before in ritual, continues to move before and around me as a shimmering and undulating opalescent or iridescent form, rippling with rainbow colors. This continues throughout the five minutes of breathing to quiet the mind.

Upon assuming the posture, I feel a powerful sensation in my right heel and observe a snake entering my body there, slithering up my right leg to my right hip. At my hip, the snake gnaws away the debris or material there, making space. It feels like a healing.

From there, it joins another snake that is resting at the base of my spine. The two snakes join, head to tail, making an infinity sign as they travel up and down my spinal column, activating both hemispheres of my brain. Then there is darkness and stillness.

The next image is of myself being born as a male. I actually see two or more male lifetimes. In one I am a chubby brown baby boy crawling across a dirt floor. Next, I have a sensation or experience of time inverted and see myself hanging upside down. I position myself in the posture of the tarot card Hanged Man and after a time a chrysalis spins around me of golden shimmering silken thread, which hardens and becomes a cocoon. From this state, I see next an intergalactic counsel where I sit without taking on a human form.

From here it is apparent that I have many descendants and see the lifetime of a Medicine Man in the jungle working plant medicine with black jaguar and condor as animal allies. I am then a benevolent king, and finally I emerge in a purple-green light as a female incarnation. I become the first priestess of this line.

In the next image, I am an elder, blind in my right eye, and I am told this is to remember the sacred ways. I sit on a rolled out woven basket on a wagon to bless the village people with my essence. I no longer speak and barely move, if at all. As the drumming slows, this journey ends.

Donna Journeys in the World of the Spirits

Donna again resonates with the Kundalini. The snakes slithering up and down the spine activate the hemispheres of the brain and the purple and green colors related to the chakra, bringing alive the magic of the upper chakra from the green of the heart to the purple of the crown. This again brings energy to her Ka Body symbolized by the infinity sign. With the inverted time and the Tarot Hanged Man of wisdom, intuition, and divination, Donna is wrapped in silken threat to become a cocoon that hatches to become a spiritual being and part of an intergalactic counsel.

She is reborn as a male for several lifetimes to become a medicine man of the jungle plant world and the benevolent king, with the purple and green light of the upper chakra. She then incarnates as a Goddess/Priestess among her many descendants. In her last image, she is a male elder with a blind right eye, like the image of the Nordic God of Gods, Odin, who became blind in his right eye on his journey for wisdom.

The question again arises, what does this have to do with the story of Jacob who becomes Israel, whose descendants become a great nation? Jacob, struggling with the angel of the Lord, refuses to let go. The angel then blesses him and gives him a new name: Israel. Though Israel remains in the physical world, Donna goes beyond the physical world and into her spirit body of the spirit world. She becomes a sacred Goddess/Priestess of this new world to bless the village people. Her Goddess-Consciousness, the internal Goddess, comes alive within her as she journeys into the new world.

Lauren

Using the Jama Coaque Metamorphosis Posture, I am a woman walking in the brush wearing colorful, flowing clothes and a garland of flowers in my hair. I get stuck in some pricker bushes. As I try to disentangle my clothes, which are tearing, I notice something watching me. I assume it's a puma, and I'm frightened. I slow down, trying not so show my fear. My clothes are now torn, and my bare feet are bleeding. There are prickers along this trail, so I wouldn't be able to run in my bare, bleeding feet even if I could free my clothes quickly.

I send out a silent call for help and then realize that the animal is a bear. He comes to me and gently removes the prickers from my clothes. Then he takes my hand and leads me to his cave.

The cave is warm and comforting. I look into his eyes to thank him and see love and gentleness there. He offers to have me hibernate with him. I want to stay and receive his warmth and comfort, but I'm hungry and know I need to leave to find food. I'm concerned about the pending cold. Bear offers to shed his fur for me. I won't let him do that, but I am grateful for his offer.

I become an eagle and fly out of the cave. It's cold in the sky. Soaring is nice, but I don't like it up here. I feel lonely and hungry. I could swoop down and eat a squirrel or a rat like eagles do, but that disgusts to me. I want to find my people but don't remember anything about them. I long for the warmth of a fire and a good meal with my people. But who are they?

I pray to God/Goddess, my higher self, my guide, my guiding angels to send me home if I have one or send me to kind people who will help me. But why can't I remember? Why was I traveling alone? I sense there has been some sort of trauma.

Now I'm back in my woman's body and clothes, cold and hungry, in the thicket. I'm fairly well hidden, and not far away I see a native tribe. They're preparing for a celebration. I can smell the game cooking over a fire. They're preparing to dance around the fire. Some already are, but things haven't gotten started yet. I don't dare expose myself. What if they hate white people? Will I become their slave?

A young man who has wandered away from the group has noticed me. He sees the fear in my eyes. His eyes are kind. He produces a bear skin and places it around my shoulders. I am grateful to him and to the bear who gave his life.

The kind young man leads me to his teepee, and I wait there for him. He brings a cup of broth and some nourishing food for me to eat. Then he leaves again. As I eat, I think about my people, whoever they are. I want to tell my people to be kind to the natives and leave them in peace. I don't know who to tell, and realize they wouldn't listen, anyway. I can't prevent the pending genocide. I can only be present in this moment, be grateful for the food and warmth, and deeply appreciate those who have helped me.

The Vow to Return Home

In my trance journey, as with Lauren's journey with Jacob, I was called to follow the Gestalt way of interpretation. Earlier I said I would usually not attempt to interpret other people's trance experiences because there are many levels of interpretation that they need to consider and live with, but when following a story like the seven stories of Genesis that provide a framework for interpretation, I feel the freedom to provide my interpretations. With these interpretations, I feel like Joseph in making his interpretations of dreams.

Following the Gestalt method, I focused on the feels exhibited by Lauren in each part of her personal journey, and then ask, "What part of the Jacob story did these feelings reflect?" Beginning with Lauren being entangled in the thornbush, where was Jacob entangled? The deception that he and his mother imposed on Isaac certainly entangled him. While entangled, she heard noises that frightener her. Rebekah and Jacob were frightened by Esau's threats of harm to Jacob, so Rebekah sent him to safety to live with her brother, Laban.

When calling out for help, a gentle bear came to Lauren to take her to his cave where he gave her warmth and comfort, but in her hunger, she needed to continue her journey to search for food. Jacob, in his dream of the ladder to heaven, found reassurance that the land of his father was his, and his offspring will be like the dust of the Earth and spread abroad. So, Jacob found comfort in having to leave home, vowing to return to his father's house in peace. Vowing this, he continued his journey.

Lauren then became an Eagle to fly in search of her home. Feeling cold, hungry, and lonely, she prayed to the God or Goddess and returned to be entangled in the thicket as herself. She saw a native tribe preparing to celebrate while dancing around a fire and preparing to eat, but she was afraid to show herself, so she hid from this nearby celebration. Following this entanglement and fear, when Jacob got to his uncle's he saw Rachel by the water tending their sheep. They fell in love, but Rachel's father, Laban, said Jacob had to serve him for seven years before they could marry. The seven years seemed like a few days, but then Laban brought her older sister, Leah, to him and said that the older daughter should marry first. So, in this entanglement with Laban, Jacob served him for another seven years before he could have the hand of Rachel.

Fearing his inability to return home as he vowed, the entanglement continued. What of Laban's livestock did Jacob deserve for his

14 years of service? This entanglement lasted for another six years, before Jacob and his family left for Canaan, leaving when Laban was away, so without his knowing.

But one man of the tribe saw Lauren entangled and came to her rescue, inviting her into his community with warmth, food, and compassion, just as the reunion of Jacob and Esau at the Jordan River was one of hugs, kisses, and acceptance. Thus, Jacob fulfilled his vow to return home to the Promised Land in the Garden of a compassionate indigenous tribe, not a place of conflict and dissention as in the world of patriarchy.

Henning

I am in the Jama Coaque Metamorphosis Posture while watching Jacob, the deceiver, from a distance as he settles by the river Jordan, preparing himself to meet his brother Esau on the following day after 20 years of absence from his father's lands and his vow to return to the home of his father. He is weary of being chased by his uncle and from a life of desire for always wanting more, for wanting his father Isaac's blessing (i.e., inheritance), for a woman, for children, and for peace after having cheated people and they cheated him. I am an eagle, perched at a distance on a hilltop, watching Jacob wrestle with God (in the guise of a man) for the entire night by the riverbank to become 'Israel.' On the next day, he dances child-like with his brother, relieved, humbled, and grateful for being forgiven by Esau and for the familial love coming even to him.

Recalling the story of Jacob's ladder, an angel of the Lord descending the ladder tells Jacob that his descendants shall spread abroad in all directions, and his descendants shall be blessed. Occupation of Israel has repeatedly changed over the centuries, causing much suffering and tears, but wherever the descendants of Abraham dwell will be the Promised Land.

With every sunrise and sunset, a century passes as I, an eagle, observe water, forests, and many people appearing on the land, then disappear again after a few days. Yet, a few days later, the whole drama repeats, a coming and going of civilizations over the ages. I cry a tear for all the suffering caused by those who suffer from the constant need for more. I take flight to circle the earth for a few centuries of observation, content and grateful for the updraft that carries me.

Israel is Wherever the Descendants of Abraham Dwell
Journeying with Jacob, Henning, as an Eagle, observes from above when Jacob faces his brother, Esau, at the crossing of the Jordan River as he vowed to return to the home of his father, Isaac. Jacob made this vow in response to the words of the Angel of the Lord in his dream of Jacob's Ladder.

Then Henning's experience continues: "With every sunrise and sunset a century passes as I observe water, forests, and many people appearing on the land. They disappear again after a few 'days,' and yet a few days later, the whole drama repeats." The question thus arises, "What is the Promised Land?" Over the centuries, the occupation of what is Israel has repeatedly changed and caused much suffering and tears. The descendants of Jacob have spread abroad to all corners of the Earth, and Israel is wherever the descendants of Abraham dwell, the New Garden, the Promised Land, the land of Our Earth Mother, our Goddess-Consciousness who dwells within each of us.

Lonnie

My mind takes a while to settle. The drumming starts, and eventually I am on a carousel riding a horse, trying to get the ring with no success. Now I am Jama Coaque, sitting on top of the mountain. It is sweltering. People are coming up to me with offerings and prayers. They seem much happier when finished and they leave. When everyone is gone, I turn

into an enormous bird and fly up into the sky until it is dark.
I land on a branch of a tree and look down on the earth.

A Journey of Frustration that Ends in Victory

Lonnie's two-part experience lent itself again to the Gestalt method of interpretation, first of his ride on the carousel, and then of his mountaintop experience. On the carousel, he failed to grab the ring, going round and round, getting nowhere, trapped in frustration. Lauren's entanglement experience of Jacob with Laban, and the frustration of not getting the ring is like Jacob's vow to return home and his inability to leave the repeated, circular barriers put up by Laban. But when Jacob escaped the carousel ride with Laban, he was welcomed home with warmth and affection, a mountaintop experience of love and acceptance. The acceptance of his descendants who turned to him with offerings and prayers was an experience that allowed him to fly high above the New World, the World of our Mother Goddess, our Goddess-Consciousness within.

Nick

I journeyed three times with Jacob using the Jama Coaque Posture. At the time of my review of Matthew Wood's book, I experience hanging onto a rope and feel someone pulling from the other end. I move along the rope, hand over hand, to see where it is taking me. I cross a small stream and then up a hill to the mouth of a cave. The rope goes into the cave as I follow it. I soon see a bear at the other end of the rope. He is laughing at me in a good-natured way. I sit down with him and can feel his strength flowing into me.

Finding Strength in Facing My Adversary

My experience begins with a feeling of curiosity, curious about what is at the other end of the rope. When I come to the bear, I am for a moment afraid because of his laughter, but then I feel strong with his good-natured manner. My focus was on Esau coming in exhausted from his work in the field. Knowing that he is starving, I am curious about how he will react when I ask him for his birthright. For a moment he is angry like a big, hairy bear, but then he shrugs his shoulders and laughs, saying, 'What use do I have for the birthright? It is yours.' I feel new strength in that I have his birthright and for standing up to him.

The second solo journey of communing with Jacob was quite similar. While using the same posture, I am again hanging onto a rope and follow it. It takes me across a river where I see an eagle's nest high in a tree. A feather floats down to land at my feet and I pick it up and cherish it. I can feel it telling me to rise above my fear as I look up to see the eagle rising in a thermal in the air. I rise above my fears.

Rising Above Fear

The eagle rising lifts me above my fears. Jacob, facing the fear of crossing the river to meet his brother, hangs on to the angel of the Lord in battle, lifting him to the highest point in his life as he becomes Israel.

Then my third experience is with the ecstatic trance group. When the drumming begins, I am in a struggle to become the coyote, and, at the same time a coyote was nearby laughing at me. I feel I cannot be both. This struggle goes on for most of the session. I find myself at the Taos Pueblo Festival with the Indians trying to climb the center pole to get the bag of goodies at the top. Several fat Indians cannot get up very high, but then one slender man gets to the top and the bag of goodies. A couple of clowns wander through the crowd, snatching the purses of several women as I watch. I feel very anxious and uncomfortable. Will they get their purses back? I cannot laugh at the clowning. Then I remember in junior high school when two boys grabbed my cap and were playing keep away with it and how humiliated I felt.

I look at the story of Jacob and feel the struggle he has with the angel and that he is comfortable to go with the flow in the struggle by hanging on. I want to feel comfortable to go with the flow and hang on.

I felt accepted twenty years ago when I was in my successful practice as a psychologist where I used the alternate reality of hypnosis. This journey in alternate reality has continued smoothly and taken me into the use of ecstatic trance. I value the ecstatic experiences, but there are some people I have been close to who think what I am doing with trance is crazy. I am not laughing at or with them but feel confident in what I am doing, and I wish they could see the value and understand the reality of ecstatic trance.

Jacob feels and believes he is doing right in returning to the home of his father, but there is anxiety in reuniting with his brother, the struggle he is facing in crossing the Jordan River. He was comfortable when he was just going with the flow rather than bucking the system, but it's too late for him to turn back and he is doing the right thing in returning home.

Overcoming Feelings of Humiliation

When others feel the control of patriarchy and have power over me, I feel humiliated. Laban had this control over Jacob, having control over what Jacob wanted, that is the hand of Rachel in marriage and gaining the livestock that was due to him. Only when he showed the strength to hang on as he hung on to the angel of the Lord, the patient strength of the love of our Great Mother, the Goddess within, did he gain what he was due and what he wanted.

Ecstatic Revelations of Jacob

First, four of the group, Donna, Lauren, Lonnie, and my experience of facing Jacob's struggle with Laban and the Angel of the Lord, overcame the feeling of entanglement and hung on to return to his father's home, the Promised Land of love and compassion of our Great Earth Mother, the Goddess-within, who dwells within each of us, and not the land of conflict and dissention of the patriarchal world.

Henning had a very different and important experience that offers a way to bring peace to the world. He found that the "Promised Land" is the land wherever the descendants of Abraham dwell. In Jacob's dream of Jacob's Ladder, the angel promised him the land where he slept. The Promised Land stretched to all corners of the Earth, to the east, south, west, and north, the New Garden where all can live in peace.

CHAPTER 10

Joseph

The Story of Joseph

Joseph, born of Rachel and Jacob, was conceived when Jacob worked for his uncle, Laban, the father of Rachel, as told in the previous chapter, the story of Jacob. After twenty years of living with Laban, Jacob returns across the Jordan River with his twelve sons and one daughter to the land of his father, Isaac, and grandfather, Abraham. Rachel dies giving birth to Benjamin, her second son. Being the first born of Rachel, Jacob loves Joseph above all others, and in his old age he makes Joseph a robe of many colors.

At seventeen years of age, Joseph was to help his brothers in pasturing their flock, but his brothers hate him because of their father's special love for him. Then Joseph has a dream: "We are binding sheaves in the field, and behold, my sheaf rises and stands upright as your sheaves gather around and bow down to my sheaf." His brothers, hearing this, hate him even more. He then had another dream: "Behold, the sun, the moon and eleven stars are bowing down to me." Telling this to his father and brothers, his father rebukes him saying, "Shall I, your mother, and your brothers indeed come to bow ourselves to the ground before you?"

His brothers are pasturing their flock in a distant pasture, and Jacob asks Joseph to go to help them. When his brothers see him coming, they conspire to kill their dreamer brother, but Reuben says, "Let us not take his life. Shed no blood but throw him in the pit." So, his brothers strip him of his robe of many colors and throw him into the pit with no water.

As they sit down to eat, they see an Ishmaelite caravan on its way to Egypt carrying gum, balm, and myrrh. They decide to sell Joseph as a slave to the caravan, for which they receive 20 shekels of silver. The brothers dip the robe in the blood of a goat and take it to their father who, when seeing it refuses to be comforted in mourning.

In Egypt, the Ishmaelites sell Joseph to the captain of the Pharaoh's guard. The Lord is with Joseph, and he becomes successful in the house of his Egyptian master and his master makes him overseer of the household. Being handsome, his master's wife seeks to lie with him, but he refuses. Once when he is with her, she catches him by his garment as he flees from the house, leaving his garment in her hand. She then calls to the men of her household, accusing Joseph of lying with her. The master, thus angered, puts Joseph in prison.

Joseph soon gains the favor of his prison keepers and they put him in charge of the prisoners because the Lord is with him. Later, two officers of the Pharaoh, his cupbearer, and the chief baker, become prisoners and prison keepers appoint Joseph to attend to them. One night they both have troubling dreams that Joseph interprets. The cupbearer dreams: "There is a vine before me with three branches. As soon as it buds, its blossoms shoot forth, and the clusters ripen into grapes. I have the Pharaoh's cup, press the grapes into the cup, and place it in the Pharaoh's hand." Joseph interprets the dream: "The three branches are three days. In three days, Pharaoh will lift your head and restore you to your office, and you shall place Pharaoh's cup in his hand as you did when you were his cupbearer."

When the chief baker sees that the interpretation was favorable, he tells Joseph his dream: "There are three cake baskets on my head, and in the uppermost basket there are many baked foods for the Pharaoh, but the birds are eating them out of the basket." Joseph answers, "The three baskets are three days. In three days, Pharaoh will lift your head and hang you from a tree, and the birds will eat the flesh from you." The third day was the Pharaoh's birthday, and he provides a feast for all his servants, lifting the head of

the chief cupbearer and the head of the chief baker. He restores the
chief cupbearer to his position but hangs the chief baker, as Joseph
interpreted.

After two years, the Pharaoh dreams he is standing by the Nile,
and behold, there comes up out of the Nile seven cows, attractive
and plump, and they feed on the reed grass. And behold, seven
other cows, ugly and thin, come up out of the Nile after them, and
stand by the other cows. The ugly, thin cows eat the seven attractive
cows. Then the Pharaoh has a second dream: "Behold, seven ears of
grain, plump and good, are growing on one stalk. Then seven ears
sprout, thin and blighted by the east wind. The thin ears swallow
up the seven plump and full ears." Troubled in the morning, the
Pharaoh calls for his magicians and all his wise men, but there is
none who can interpret the dreams. The chief cupbearer, though,
remembers Joseph's ability to interpret dreams, thus the pharaoh
calls for him. Joseph says that it is not from me, but God will give
you a favorable answer: "Your dreams are one; God has revealed to
you what is about to happen. The seven good cows and the seven
good ears are seven years of plenty. The seven lean and ugly cows
and the seven empty ears blighted by the east wind are seven years
of famine. There will come seven years of great plenty throughout
Egypt, but after them there will arise seven years of famine, and the
years of plenty will be forgotten. The doubling of the dream means
God fixed it and will shortly bring it about. Let Pharaoh appoint
overseers over the land to take one-fifth of the produce of the land
and store it during the seven years of plenty. The overseers shall
reserve the food for the seven years of famine so that all may not
perish throughout the famine."

This proposal pleases Pharaoh, so he says to Joseph, "Since God
has shown you all this, there is none so discerning and wise as you.
You shall be over my house, and my people shall do as you command. Only as regards the throne will I be greater than you." The
Pharaoh takes his signet ring from his hand and puts it on Joseph's
finger, clothes him in garments of fine linen, and put a gold chain

about his neck. Thus, Joseph becomes the governor over the land, and the land prospers for seven years, with one fifth of what the Earth provides stored for the time of famine.

Then come the seven years of famine and Joseph doles out the food that was saved to fulfill the needs of the people of Egypt. But the day comes when the brothers of Joseph hear Egypt has sufficient food, so they go to Egypt to buy what they needed. Joseph recognizes his brothers, but they do not recognize him, and he treats them like strangers. Jacob kept Benjamin at home, fearing that the Egyptians might enslave him. After some time of questioning and testing about their father, Benjamin and dead brother, Joseph accuses them of being spies and puts them in custody for three days. In prison, they think that this distress was because of what they had done to their brother, Joseph. They do not know that Joseph understands their Hebrew because of his use of an interpreter. But then Joseph sends them home with sacks of food, and he has the money they came with for buying the food also placed in the sacks.

Returning to the home of their father, they tell him all that had happened and find the money in the sacks. After a year, the food supplies again run out and the brothers need to return to Egypt to buy more. Jacob again does not want to send Benjamin as Joseph had insisted, but in the end, because of the severe famine and the brothers' pledge for Benjamin's safety, Benjamin joins them on their return trip. They take with them double the money and other gifts.

When Joseph sees Benjamin, he orders his servants to prepare a feast. The brothers fear Joseph's steward will accuse them of stealing the money placed in the sacks and they hesitate to enter the house, but the steward assures them, saying, "Peace to you, do not be afraid." He brings them into the house and gives them water to wash their feet and fodder for their donkeys. When Joseph comes to greet them, they bow down to the ground before him. Joseph asks about the health of Jacob. When Joseph sees Benjamin, he must hurry out because of his need to cry. When he returns, he and the brothers are served separately because the Egyptians cannot eat with the Hebrews, for that is an abomination to the Egyptians, but as the brothers sit before Joseph, they look at one another in amazement. They drink and are merry.

Joseph orders his steward to fill their sacks, to return their money and in Benjamin's sack to put Joseph's cup of silver. In the morning, they leave to return to their father. After they have gone a short distance, Joseph orders his steward to overtake them and ask, "Why have you repaid good with evil?" He accuses them of stealing Joseph's silver cup. Whoever has the cup will be Joseph's servant and the rest will be innocent. The brothers quickly lower their sacks and open them. When the steward finds the cup in Benjamin's sack, they all tear their clothes in grief, return to the city, and fall to the ground before Joseph. Judah speaks but does not know what to say other than we are all your servants. Joseph says, "Only the man who had the cup shall be my servant. The rest of you go in peace to your father." Judah says, "The boy cannot leave his father, for his father would die. Take me as your servant so the boy can return to his father."

Joseph cries and orders everyone to leave. He weeps aloud, such that the household of the Pharaoh hears him. Joseph then calls his brothers to him and says, "I am your brother, Joseph, whom you sold as a slave into Egypt, but do not distress because God sent me before you to preserve life." His brothers cannot answer in their dismay. He tells them, "Hurry and go to our father and tell him that God has made me lord of Egypt. Tell him to come to me, and you shall dwell in the Land of Goshen, the best land in Egypt. You and your children and your children's children, and your flocks, your herds, and all that you have shall dwell near me. I will provide for you, for there are yet five years of famine to come. Hurry and bring our father." He kisses all his brothers and weeps upon them. The Pharaoh, hearing this is pleased, and tells them to take wagons for your little ones and wives. To each one he gives a change of clothes but to Benjamin he gives three hundred shekels of silver and five changes of clothes.

So, they return to the land of Canaan and their father, telling him that Joseph is still alive and ruler over all the land of Egypt. And God speaks to Jacob in visions of the night and says, "Jacob, Jacob. Here I am. I am God, the God of your father. Do not be afraid to go down to Egypt, for there I will make you into a great nation. I will go down with you to Egypt, and I will also bring you up again, and Joseph's hand shall close your eyes." So, the sons of Israel carry Jacob, their little ones, and wives and all they have in the wagons of the Pharaoh to the Land of Goshen. Joseph prepares his chariot and goes to meet them in Goshen. He falls on his father's neck and weeps, and Jacob says, "Now let me die, since I have seen your face and know that you are alive."

Joseph tells his brothers, "When the Pharaoh asks of your occupation, tell him your servants have been keepers of livestock from our youth even until now in order that we may dwell in the land of Goshen for every shepherd is an abomination to the Egyptians." When coming before the Pharaoh, they tell him that "We sojourn in this land for there is no pasture for our servants' flocks, for the famine is severe in the land of Canaan. And now, please let our servants dwell in the land of Goshen." The Pharaoh says to Joseph, "Your father and your brothers have come to you. The land of Egypt is before you. Settle your father and your brothers in the best of the land. Let them settle in the land of Goshen, and if you know any able men among them, put them in charge of my livestock." Then Joseph brings Jacob before the Pharaoh and Jacob blesses him.

The famine continues in its severity, so Joseph buys the livestock from the people to be added to the Pharaoh's herd in exchange for food, and when that runs out the next year, he buys the land for the Pharaoh and the people become his servants. Joseph then provides them with seed to be sown on the land, and at the time of harvest they are to give a fifth to the Pharaoh. The Israelites on the Land of Goshen are fruitful and multiply. Jacob lives in Egypt for 17 years to the age of 147 years and before the time of his death he asks Joseph not to bury him in Egypt but return him to the land of Abraham. And Joseph brings to Jacob his two sons who were born in Egypt and Jacob blesses them, knowing that the younger son will be greater than the older, putting Ephraim before Manasseh. He then says, "I am about to die, but God will be with you and will bring you again to the land of your fathers, and you will have the mountain slope I took from the hand of the Amorites with my sword and bow."

Jacob calls together his sons to tell them of their future. After Reuben who he says would not have preeminence, he goes to Simeon and Levi and because of their weapons of violence they will not be in the council for in their anger they killed men. He continues down the line to describe to each son telling them of their future. He then tells Joseph that the Almighty blesses him. Jacob then dies and is embalmed as the Egyptians and the Egyptians weep, and they return him to the land of Canaan where he is buried.

At 110 years of age, Joseph tells his brothers that God will visit them and bring them up out of this land to the land that he swore to Abraham, to Isaac and to Jacob/Israel. Joseph then dies and they embalm and bury him in Egypt.

The generations of Israel remained in Egypt for 430 years until Moses returns them to Israel.

*

Now are the stories of the five of us in the ecstatic trance group standing in the Venus of Galgenberg Posture (Fig. 10.1), a spirit journey posture that will carry us into the sky world. It is a 32,000-year-old figurine found along the Danube River near Krems, Austria. It is the oldest posture we use.

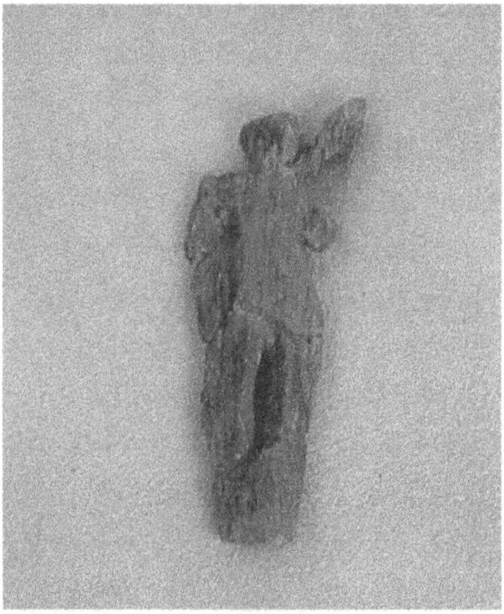

Fig. 10.1

Donna

During the breathing to quiet the mind, I sense beings gathering around me. They gently stroke my face and undulate towards me in waves that focus as they approach. Suddenly, I feel something pop into my mouth. It is flat, thin, and beige or brown. I imagine it is a wafer, but upon writing this I am hearing in my head it was a stone. Either way, it feels like a sacrament of sorts.

As I assume the Venus of Galgenberg Posture, my body sways, then it rotates counterclockwise. My arm feels strained, and I adjust it intermittently but continue to keep it elevated. I sense water all around me. Being on the water, I see canoes floating nearby. They are wooden and have tall, curved bows fore and aft, carved with symbols and possibly painted. Then a pair of brilliant blue eyes appears before me, framed by a fur-trimmed hood or hat. This being is male, robust, and in his power. The feeling is jovial, and I hear a hearty laugh. We are about to embark on a fishing expedition. We are heading out to hunt and there are other men around us. The environment of the Baltic Sea is cold and sunny. The clothing is thick woolen with fur parkas with colorful embroidered trimming.

The Sacred World of the North

The first six stories of Genesis, from Adam and Eve to Jacob, Donna's experiences were harbingers of the story of Joseph and his ability to interpret dreams. Though in Joseph's journey he found himself twice sold as a slave and imprisoned, with each trauma, he had the self-confidence to rise above the potential for experiencing the traumas with the pain of self-defeat. With his self-confidence and ability to interpret dreams, he eventually became governor of Egypt with only the Pharaoh above him in authority. He rose to and above his crown chakra with the energy of entering the world of the spirits, a world that Donna entered as she has grown through each of her experiences to become one with her Goddess-Consciousness that is within her.

In this concluding experience in journeying with Joseph, Donna came to it sacramentally in feeling gentle strokes of caressing energy and in taking a sacramental stone that popped in her mouth. This journey then took her to the far north surrounded by canoes and the water of the Baltic Sea, where she met a beautiful and jovial fisherman with a hearty laugh. In this unexpected setting, she joined the men in their fishing expedition in the cold but sunny north, suggesting that the Promised Land, the New Garden, is anywhere that the descendants of Abraham exist, in Egypt, the world of Joseph, and even in the far north where Donna can continue her journey with the spirits.

Lauren

I'm standing in the uncomfortable Venus of Galgenberg Posture, but my body needs to move to the beat of the drum. I am in Medina, Egypt with people everywhere. My arm is in the air, and I am dancing. I look like a court jester wearing pointy shoes and a silly hat that looks like a droopy crown with bells on it. I feel playful and free.

Joseph is there. I ask him how he interprets the dreams. He says it's not by knowing what the dreams have to say about the future. It's by telling a story about the dream, and in this way, he is speaking the future into existence. The baker was mixing and creative, so he got to live. The butcher was cutting and separating, thus he needed to die.

Sometimes I was a cat in this Egyptian Medina. Sometimes I was Joseph and the jester simultaneously. Joseph says the secret to his success is playfulness, like a child. Children don't see the differences of separation until they're taught to do so. They are creative geniuses. Because he didn't have the usual adult conflicts within him, he didn't have external conflicts. He loved and forgave everyone, and everyone loved and accepted him.

Joseph never spoke of God. There were no parents pitting against children in his story. I don't remember him ever calling on God for support. And he certainly didn't do so out of vengeance.

There was also a scene in my experience about an African tribesman. He had red and white paint on his face. He carried a spear. I was no longer a court jester, but a woman, open and centered like Joseph. I asked him where his people were. We didn't speak the same language, but we communicated telepathically. He said they're around, hiding, watching, and waiting. They are ready to fight if need be. I knew there would be no fight, and that these people would grow to accept me. We danced, but not around a bonfire. It's hot in Africa.

This wasn't about Joseph. It was about the tribe. I moved and danced throughout the entire experience. I was too uncomfortable not to do so.

The Sacred World of Africa

In this Venus of Galgenberg Posture, Lauren feels the posture of dance, of moving playfully as a silly clown with bells, playfully free. The lesson she learns to carry her to her highest level, her Goddess-Consciousness, is that Joseph looked to the dreams to tell a story, the story playfully speaking the future into existence with the playfulness and freedom of a child. The child lives in the world of creative genius, not having the usual adult conflicts of separation. Joseph did not see the traumas of life negatively but as opportunities to rise to higher positions in life. He loved and forgave everyone and was loved and accepted by all.

Lauren, taking on Joseph's attitude toward life, met an African tribesman ready to fight if need be. But with her new matriarchal attitude of love and compassion, she joined in the dance in a circle, dancing in a playful, silly, childlike manner, free of the conflicts of adulthood. Again, like Donna who found the spirits of her spirit world in the Baltic north, Lauren finds the spirits of the spirit world in Africa, her Promised Land, the world of innocence that is found everywhere in the new Garden of Eden.

Henning

I stand in the Venus of Galgenberg Posture. Joseph is my name. I lose everything when my brothers throw me in the pit and sell me as a slave. I am exiled, and no connection to my former life remains except for what I strongly sense as a silver thread linking me to my father, Jacob.

Why no connection to my mother? This story, as all the previous ones, do not ascribe a role of importance to women, to the world of matriarchy. Women are possessions, temptresses, or breeding pods. I don't want to dwell on the societal war of patriarchy and let it go. So be it and let the story flow.

I cross a river with the caravan of merchants who bought me, which marks a final shedding of all that was familiar. But I am not desperate, having received the grace of God, the grace of foresight: "The sun, the moon, and 11 stars, my family, will bow to me." Thus, I know I am not doomed. I have tasks to accomplish in the face of adversity. From the pit, I rise to status in a household; I lose it all and am thrown into a dungeon on false accusations. I foresee famine and save many peoples' lives, rising to the highest office next to only the Pharaoh. But of most importance, I save my family's souls, specifically my brothers' souls through forgiveness, all simply because God has given me the grace of faith, letting doubt fall by the wayside.

My arm trembles from the physical strain of holding the Venus of Galgenberg Posture. My attention shifts to the sun and moon orbiting on opposite sides, around me for a while. The sun exerts itself in shining, and the moon receives the light. Children don't know separation until taught. At the very end, as the drum beat changes, I sense the distinct smell of Rape', an Amazonian snuff based on a type of tobacco (Nicotiana Rustica), tree ash and herbs.

Henning's Empathetic Feelings

Henning, as Joseph loses everything when thrown in the pit and then sold as a slave. Crossing the river into Egypt is the shedding of all that was familiar. Yet, Joseph, saved from doom by being graced by God with foresightful knowledge, has tasks to accomplish in facing the adversity he experiences. With this knowledge, he rises to the highest office next only to the Pharaoh. His grace of love and forgiveness for his brothers brings him the orbiting light from the sun and its reflection on the moon.

As with Donna and Lauren, and Henning's previous experience with Jacob, he too discovers the Promised Land beyond Israel, and wherever his head lies in sleep. The Promised Land is where the descendants of Abraham dwell.

With this dissolution of the separation of Israel and Palestine, peace comes as Henning returns to the Garden, the new Promised Land, the Land of peace and the acceptance of diversity that overcomes the separation of good and evil. Henning takes his intense ability to feel empathy in each of his experiences into the Garden, empathy of the matriarch that ends the separation of good and evil and brings the people together in mutual understanding. Thus, in the matriarchal world, the love of the compassionate Goddess within continues to grow to bring Henning to a higher-level consciousness.

Lonnie

I stand erect in the Venus of Galgenberg Posture holding the earth. Its weight is unbearable. I put my arm down to my side and immediately feel relief. Now I am in the desert. I'm in a jeep with a large machine gun mounted in the back. There are people on either side of me. They look scared seeing the gun. I pull the trigger and flowers come out, then water. Suddenly, the desert turns lush green. Then it is winter. There are trees that grow and smoke coming from chimneys. I can see people inside. They are eating, drinking, and dancing. I feel happy. My work is done. Now I put my arms back up and hold the world. It feels so much lighter.

Fear and Celebration

The weight of the Earth is unbearable. The jeep with its machine gun frightens the people around Lonnie, but when he pulls the trigger and flowers and water come out, turning the desert to a lush green, bringing celebration.

Then the scene changes. It is winter with grown trees and smoke coming from chimneys. The people are eating, drinking, and dancing in celebration, the celebration continuing in places beyond the desert of Egypt, places of the Promised Land, the New Garden. Lonnie's love and compassion continues to grow, bring him more and more into the world of matriarchy and his Goddess-Consciousness within him.

Nick

At the time of my review of the book by Matthew Wood, I had the following experience using the Venus of Galgenberg Posture.

I am traveling with Joseph in the caravan towards Egypt, interpreting dreams. When we get to Egypt, I am thrown in prison where I continue to interpret dreams until the Pharaoh calls upon me to interpret his dreams. I became popularly accepted for my ability, which saved Egypt from seven years of famine.

I come from the land of my father, Canaan/Israel, the land of my people given to them by their visions of their God, but my dreams tell me that my people are of lands much bigger than those that were of the land of Israel. My people are those of the world who value their dreams and the ability to journey in the other world.

The people of Israel have thought of me as being in exile in the land of Egypt, but Egypt and the world are my home. The Pharaoh welcomes me and my family to the fertile land of Goshen and my ability to turn the desert green. Through the last four stories, Abraham and his descendants live in continued battle with the Canaanites whose land they see as given them by their visions of God, a world of separation. Welcomed in the land of Egypt by the Pharaoh because of Joseph's connection with the other world, the world of our Great Mother Earth, he is at home in this Promised Land. His connection to the other world ends the world of separation, the separation of knowledge of good and evil.

The Promised Land is Where the Descendants of Abraham Dwell

My first Joseph experience at the time I reviewed Matthew Wood's book was several months before the group ecstatic trance sessions, and I did not tell the group of my earlier experiences. Yet, this experience was much like Henning's Jacob experience and the experience of journeying with Joseph for the rest of the group. My journey takes me through the story of Joseph and his coming from the land of his father, Israel/Canaan, but my ecstatic dream tells me that my people are from many other places than those living in the land of Israel/Canaan. The descendants of Abraham find the Promised Land wherever they dwell. Joseph, exiled in the land of Egypt and welcomed by the Pharaoh, Egypt became his home, his Promised Land, while in Canaan they were in continued battle with the Canaanites. The Promised Land is the world of our Great Mother Earth.

Then, with the ecstatic trance group using the Venus of Galgenberg Posture I had the following experience: At first, I felt myself as Joseph flying like superman over Egypt, checking on the fields of the Egyptian farmers who were supposed to give one fifth of what they grew to Joseph for storage to be used during the years of famine.

Then I became the youthful Black Bear, whom I met in Pennsylvania, who found several eagle nests and from below these nests he gathered eagle feathers dropped to him, feathers that became part of his eagle dance costume. With his ability to see beyond his five senses, he became important to the tribe in leading the hunt. Black Bear's ability to see where they would find deer and other game on the hunt brought him to his leadership role. I quickly realized that my/his out-stretched arm gave him the ability to see, and when he lowered it, the hunters were where they found the game for their success on the hunt.

Both Joseph and Black Bear have ways of seeing beyond their five senses, Joseph in his dreams and Black Bear in his trance visions. This ability gives them power among their people, Black Bear as a shaman, and Joseph as the Governor of Egypt. Their authority sets them apart from the rest of the people, the people of the village or country. They have an important position in the coming New Age, the power of seeing beyond their five senses.

The World of Seeing Beyond the Five Senses

Again, my second experience in journeying with Joseph was self-evident. After a brief visit to Joseph surveying the land of Egypt, I find myself in Pennsylvania where I have had several previous experiences as Black Bear, a Lenni Lenape. He has the power to see just as Joseph has in interpreting dreams, and he becomes a respected shaman of his tribe just as Joseph does in becoming Governor of Egypt. His ability to see beyond his five senses is an important power or ability in the coming New Age, the return to the innocence and the ways of the hunter-gatherers for living in the Garden of Eden, the matriarchal worldwide garden of the New Age. The land of Central Pennsylvania is my Promised Land.

Ecstatic Revelations of Joseph

What have we learned from the story of Joseph? First, his ability to interpret dreams takes him into the new world. This ability to see beyond the five senses of sight, sound, taste, smell, and touch is an ability of the hunting and gathering matriarchal cultures as I experienced in my Joseph experience with the group. As we learn or gain this ability, we return to the world of the hunter-gathers, a return that we can call the New Age, the New Garden, or the Promised Land.

Second, each of us experienced the Promised Land as anywhere that the descendants or Abraham dwell, not specifically what the maps show as Israel. This took Donna to the area around the Baltic Sea, and Lauren to Africa. It took Henning to wherever we lay our head, Lonnie to a place in the north with trees, and me to Central Pennsylvania.

Third, facing trauma in one's life, a person can rise to new heights by holding within an attitude of self-confidence, childlike innocence, and playfulness, forgiving others with love. Adam and Eve, being born into the world in the Garden of Eden, had this childlike innocence before gaining the knowledge of good and evil which brought them into the patriarchal material world of separation in which we now live.

Finally, as we leave the patriarchal world of the off-planet God of separation, we return to the Goddess of creation, the matriarchal earth Goddess that brings together all that is of the Earth. This world is the world of our hunter-gatherer ancestors who lived in interdependency with all that is of the Earth with the love and compassion of our great Earth Goddess. This Goddess is alive within each of us, and as we begin to experience her within of us, we feel her loving compassion grow. Our Inner Goddess-Consciousness dissolves the conflict of the patriarchal world of separation, of good and evil, of us vs. them.

CHAPTER 11

Returning to the Garden

The Garden, what was and is it like? The Garden of Eden was the Garden of the innocence of creation, innocent like the innocence of a newborn child who does not know right from wrong, good from evil, or me separate from you. The Garden, as many of us think of it now, is the Garden in which the hunter and gatherers lived, a garden that provides for all our needs on the Earth of our Great Mother where all life is interdependent and sacred.

What do the five of us of the group bring to this Garden? First, when expelled from the garden we face a world of dichotomies, a world of good vs. evil, of us vs. them, a world of conflict. Each of the group found ways for dealing with these dichotomies of life through ecstatic trance. Next, our stories bring us the ability to listen beyond our five senses, beyond our perception of sight, sound, taste, smell, and touch. Before the Tower of Babel, the voice heard seemed to come from beyond ourselves, from God. After the tower, our ability to listen seemed to come from within ourselves of what we experience in our nighttime dreams, visions and in altered states of trance.

The way of the Kundalini, the cyclic journey along the spine, brings those of us entering the Garden to new levels of seeing how we can overcome the separation and conflict we experience in the modern patriarchal world. The matriarchal cycle of conception, birth, life, death, and rebirth into greater health and maturity is a cyclic journey up and down along the spine. On this journey, we grow to bring alive our Goddess-Consciousness within us at our crown chakra. Our Goddess-Consciousness brings each of us to be one with our Great Earth Mother, the creator of the Earth and all that is of the Earth, as our ancestors felt in their connection with the Earth.

Also, with the rationality of the modern world, we have lost the role of emotions that adds to our understanding of life. Emotions bring alive our experiences of life around us. And finally, the participants of this ecstatic trance group found that wherever they dwell is the Promised Land, not just the geographic country Israel, a most important message in bringing peace to the world of the Garden. These five keys to the Garden bring much deeper meaning to the Genesis Stories.

Resolving the Separation of Good and Evil

When we gained the knowledge of good and evil when expelled from the Garden of Eden, we entered the world of rationality, a dichotomous world of us vs. them, of the patriarchy's search for power and control. In this world of the last 2500 years, we struggled with how to survive with conflicts created in this world of a patriarchal God of separation. Each person of the ecstatic trance group found a fresh path through this world of conflict that leads to spiritual growth. Donna was instructed by the Earth Mother to pay no attention to the patriarchal stories but to attend to her growing Goddess-Consciousness within. Lauren danced with and learned the wisdom offered by the serpent, the serpent that was the source of wisdom for many of the ancient cultures. She found this wisdom not as comfortable as the life of innocence she experienced in the Garden of Eden, but with the help of Adam, they found the ways to survive. Henning felt confined in the Garden, and when venturing into the world of separation outside the Garden, the world that pits us against them, he could see truth in a lie, truth in both sides of the conflicts of good vs. evil, in us vs. them. Lonnie experienced the separation of loving nature versus the controllers of nature by the agriculturalists who use all that is of the Earth for profit. With this understanding he rose above this separation by appreciating the rising sun. I found resolution to this separation in honesty and in knowing that it was not a result of eating the apple, but in how I eat it, offering something in reciprocity to show my appreciation.

Listening to the Spirits

As described by Julian Jaynes, during the earliest eras of the hunter-gatherers, the voices of the spiritual world were experienced coming from outside one's body. But with evolution, what we experienced coming from outside the body is now perceived as coming from within when in an altered-state-of-consciousness such as in a dream or a trance state. Knowing the slow nature of the process of evolution, this change in brain functioning occurred early, at the time of the Tower of Babel, a tower built to reach up to be closer to God to hear again his voice. This evolution of the brain must have come much earlier during the era of the hunter-gatherers before these metaphoric stories were recorded in the Torah and later in the Old Testament. Now, this world of the spirits is best attained in a state of trance or in a dream state.

Since each experience of the five of us was heard during the state of ecstatic trance, they were experiences of Listening to the Spirits.

Donna's experience with Cain and Abel takes her into the spirit world of seeing beyond her five senses. She becomes her spirit guide, a bear coming out of hibernation. She experiences the strong spirit body of Bear connected to everything, including the stars, specifically Ursa Major. Her deep sense of Bear, her spirit guide, offers her guidance on her journey to her Goddess-Consciousness. Bear is part of everything, of all life, including its brother the Salmon. We are all one, but we have forgotten this connection to everything. God, the Cosmos, and the Bear are one, the co-creators of everything, bringing a new spiritual dimension to Donna's inner Goddess-Consciousness.

Considering Lauren's journey with Jacob, focusing on Lauren's feelings exhibited in each part of her journey, each part was of listening to Lauren's entanglement on Jacob's journey to his uncle Laban's and his return to his father. Thus, Jacob fulfilled his vow to return home just as Lauren felt the love of being part of her new indigenous community, bringing her close to the love and compassion of the Mother Goddess who lives within each person, our Goddess-Consciousness.

Henning's Jacob experience and his dream of "Jacob's Ladder," showed him that the land of Israel, the Promised Land, extends in all directions to include the entire Earth wherever the descendants of Abraham dwell.

Lonnie's Cain and Abel experience is one of going into the deepest trance, a journey into the world of the spirits, where he experiences amnesia, amnesia that prevents him from experiencing Cain's killing of Abel, a murder that would not fit with Lonnie's philosophy of life.

In listening to the spirits after Noah and the Flood, each person of the group sees this new world of the spirits from a different perspective. Donna sees its beauty in discovering the interconnection between everything of Mother Earth, while Lauren sees it as a time to learn the balance between the rational and the dream world. Henning experiences the emotion of the fear in experiencing the lack of familiarity with everything new in the world. Lonnie returns to the Earth, to a calm world with welcoming survivors. And my experience of facing a crisis such as the flood is an opportunity for personal growth. Each experience opens new doors to life and the New Garden.

In my experience with Abraham, the insightful spiritual message learned is that a sacrifice is required to overcome crises in life, the sacrifice of the Ram for Abraham, and for me, getting my legs wet to cross the stream. In my second experience as Abraham, my spirit guide, the coyote, is laughing at me in my crazy determination to sacrifice my son.

Each story offers the power gained from listening to the spirits, a power that comes alive in the New World, the Matriarchal World of returning to the Garden, the Garden of our Great Earth Mother.

Connecting to the Kundalini and our Great Earth Mother

The Alchemical Spirit Body, the Ka Body, is a duplicate of the physical body but experienced in the spirit world beyond the physical body. Bringing alive the Spirit Body takes an increase in spiritual energy that is increased as we progress from our root chakra to our crown chakra and above to bring us the light of moon and sun. Our spirit body connects us to the spirit world beyond the physical/rational world that we experience in much of today's world. This concept of the Kundalini is very ancient. It was first described as coming from Nubia and into the earliest eras of Egypt, coming from the matriarchal era of the hunter-gatherers before it ever reached India. During these ancient times, the spirit world was open to us, but now we need to be in an altered state of consciousness, whether in a dream or trance state, to reach this world of the spirits.

Donna's Adam and Eve experience takes her into this spirit world of her alchemical spirit body. Her journey first carries her into the world of the spirit with no physical sense of herself, into this non-geocentric timeless world, and the counterclockwise world different from her common perspective. In this world of alchemy, her internal alchemy is much more personal than the alchemy of turning material substances into gold. This internal alchemy turns her way of experiencing the world into gold. In this shamanic altered state of consciousness, her pierced heart lets in the light of the sun, the Egyptian sun god Ra, bringing her wisdom from beyond her physical five senses of sight, sound, taste, smell, and touch.

Donna's journey takes her into the purple blooms of the upper chakras that rely upon the strength of her yellow solar plexus chakra, and the child-like innocence of the green heart chakra. This spirit world journey is the matriarchal cycle of conception, birth, life, death, and rebirth. Beginning with conception in the darkness of the Maiden Goddess's womb at the sacral chakra, she rises to the light of birth at the crown chakra of the Great Mother Goddess. The Crone Goddess then leaves the crown chakra journeying to the darkness of death at the root chakra before the cycle is repeated with the Maiden Goddess of conception rising from the sacral chakra to rebirth at the crown chakra. This cycle is repeated with maturity and growth until her Goddess-Consciousness is reached.

Donna's journey with Abraham again brings her to her spirit body. Flying under the belly of Quetzalcoatl, the feathered serpent carries her into the heavens in a journey of transformation from her root chakra up into the spirit world. The blue energy of her throat chakra infuses in her cranial sinus cavities with a liquid energy somewhere between water/oil and fire. Her journey reflects Abraham's spirit journey of transformation that leads him to become the father of a great nation.

In Donna's journey with Isaac, she finds herself in a ritual with a group of shamans from which she emerges as a wandering nomadic mystic who the people seek to be blessed. In a cleansing ritual, a large bird pecks out her spleen, and she disappears into purple/green light, the light of her crown chakra descending from the heavens connecting her to her spirit body.

Henning also journeys through his chakra with the story of Isaac. In his struggle with the dishonesty of Sarah and Jacob in deceiving Isaac, he finds himself in his fifth chakra, the throat chakra that is the gateway of truth and breath, the gateway for the fifth story of Genesis. He feels the energy of his spirit body flowing up over his head and back down the front of his torso, carrying both the sun and the moon on opposite sides of this orbit. In inhaling the sunlight, all pores and parts of his aura body radiate all frequencies of the visible, audible and heat spectra, the spirit energy of his Ka/Spirit Body, carrying him into the new world beyond the Isaac story that remains in the physical world, bringing him closer to his inner Goddess-Consciousness.

Donna's Jacob experience again resonates with the Kundalini with the snakes slithering up and down the spine, activating the rainbow colors of the chakras, bringing alive the magic of the upper chakra and her inner Goddess-Consciousness, carrying her from the green of the heart to the purple of the crown. With this transformation, she incarnates as a Goddess/Priestess among her many descendants. Donna goes beyond the physical world into her spirit body of the spirit world, to become a sacred elder of this new world to bless the village people.

Each of these stories that brings alive the love and compassion of our Goddess-Consciousness brings alive within us our connection to our Great Earth Mother, the creator of the Earth and all that is of the Earth. Being part of our Earth Mother was central to the lives of our hunter-gathering ancestors and will be central to us as we enter the New World, the World of Time-Free Transparence.

Connecting with the World of Emotions

Dividing the earliest era of Jean Gebser's five eras of consciousness[1], the archaic era of consciousness, into three eras, the second opens a person to the brain centers for experiencing emotions that are automatic, pure, and without control. These emotions produce agreeable and disagreeable experiences, emotional experiences caused by the separation of good and evil when humans gained knowledge by eating the forbidden fruit.

As we move through these seven eras of consciousness into the sixth era of rational consciousness, emotions are thought to be a hindrance in making logical/rational decisions. But the ecstatic experiences that call upon our emotions reflect the ways of our hunter-gatherer ancestors, an important factor as we return to the Garden.

Henning, on his journey with Noah, focuses on the dove, searching for dry land after the rain ends. On his third venture, the dove finds dry land, but Henning feels miserable and afraid of the unfamiliarity of the new world. He finds comfort though by taking a dust bath in the dirt. This new world without human or animal life other than those on the Ark is an unfamiliar, fearful new beginning.

In Henning's journey with Abraham, he vividly experiences the emotions of Abraham as he faces the crises in Abraham's life.

First, he sees the barren and desolate land of the Canaanites that Abraham is about to enter as an immigrant, land that is suffering a famine. He also empathizes with Abraham's pain when he is about to sacrifice his young son Isaac, his only heir. Henning feeling the excruciating pain of this sacrifice.

In journeying with Isaac, Lonnie's loss of the sense of time and his confusion in darkness shows that he is experiencing a deepening trance, disassociating from the anxiety due to what he might discover in the darkness of his trance. Such anxiety is not uncommon and the reason that I usually offer an ego strengthening exercise before entering trance. The trauma that is frequently uncovered in trance is the source of such anxiety, and in this case is the conflict and quarreling between the two brothers, Jacob and Esau. When Lonnie sees in the shadows the two brothers quarreling, his anxiety rises, and he again disassociates by seeking to learn the time as it again becomes dark. Lonnie's nature is to avoid conflict and quarrels. He then realizes that his open mouth is an entrance to a dark tunnel that goes down his throat, the entryway to an honest, but fearful, cold, and damp tunnel. In going down the tunnel to his root chakra, he would find there his insecurities and fears, but he avoids this journey of entering the tunnel.

In the second of my three experiences with Isaac, as an eagle, I rise above my fear of prostate cancer, as Isaac rises above his fear of being sacrificed when he sees his father, Abraham, listening to the voice of the spirit and turning to sacrifice a ram. The eagle gave me a cherished gift of a feather, while Abraham received a gift from the Holy Spirit, a reprieve from sacrificing Isaac.

The Promised Land

A major world conflict is the conflict between the Israelis and the Palestinians. The Israelis believe God gave them the Promised Land of Israel. This conflict is another example of the separation of learning the knowledge of good and evil to be resolved as we return to the Garden.

Henning journeys with Jacob as an Eagle, observing from above when Jacob faces his brother Esau at the crossing of the Jordan River. Jacob makes the vow to return home to his father Isaac in response to the Angel of the Lord, telling him: "I will give to you, to your seed, and your seed's seed the land whereon you lie your head. Your descendants shall be as the dust of the earth, and they shalt spread abroad to the west, and to the east, and to the north, and to the south, and in you and, your seed, shall I bless all the families of the earth."[2] These words came to Jacob 20 years earlier in the dream of Jacob's Ladder as he slept beyond the Jordan River on the Promised Land on his journey to his Uncle Laban's.

Henning's observations continue as centuries pass, many people appear on the land, and disappear again after a few 'days,' and yet a few days later, the whole drama repeats. The question thus arises, "What is the Promised Land?" Over the centuries, the occupants of Israel have repeatedly changed and caused much suffering and tears. But hope is with the descendants of Jacob who have spread abroad to all corners of the Earth, and Israel is wherever the descendants of Abraham dwell.

The experiences of each member of the group take their Joseph experience to places other than the geographic Israel we know today.

Donna's final sacramental experience in journeying with Joseph took her to the Baltic north surrounded by canoes and water. There she met a jovial fisherman with a hearty laugh. In this unexpected setting, she joined the men in their fishing expedition, suggesting that we can find the Promised Land anywhere, in Egypt, the world of Joseph, and even in the far north where Donna can continue her journey with the spirits.

Joseph's playful and child-like attitude toward life took Lauren to Africa where she met an African tribesman ready to fight if need be. But with her Goddess-Consciousness of love for all, she joined in the dance around the dance court, dancing playfully, sillily, and in a childlike manner, free of the conflicts of adulthood. Lauren finds the spirits of the spirit world of the Promised Land in Africa, the world of innocence as found in the Garden of Eden.

In his final experience, Henning experiences Joseph's loss of everything when sold into slavery, shedding all that was familiar as he entered Egypt. Yet, graced with the foresight of knowing he would survive adversity, he had tasks to accomplish in facing his experienced trauma. With this knowledge, he rose to the highest office next to the Pharaoh. With the grace of loving and forgiving, his brothers bring him the light from the sun and its reflection on the moon orbiting the Earth. He finds the Promised Land in Egypt. The Promised Land is wherever the descendants of Abraham dwell.

In Lonnie's journey with Joseph, his jeep with the large, mounted machine gun frightens the people surrounding him, but when he pulls the trigger, flowers come out, then water, turning the desert to a lush green. The people celebrate in the greening of the land with flowers. Then, with the coming of winter, Lonnie is among growing trees and homes with smoke coming from chimneys. The people are eating, drinking, and dancing in celebration, the celebration continuing in places beyond the desert of Egypt, places of the Promised Land.

My first Joseph experience was experienced a few months before the group ecstatic trance sessions, and I did not tell the group of my earlier experiences. Yet, this experience was much like the experiences of the rest of the group. Journeying through the story of Joseph, coming from the land of his father, Israel, my experience tells me that his people are much bigger than those that were in the land of Israel. Exiled in Egypt, and welcomed by the Pharaoh, he felt at home, while in Canaan they were in continued strife and battle with the Canaanites. The Promised Land is the world beyond Israel, the world of our Great Earth Mother.

In my second experience with Joseph, I became the young Lenape, Black Bear, who I envisioned in Pennsylvania. Black Bear, in training to become a medicine man, brings the Promised Land to Pennsylvania. Both Joseph and Black Bear have ways of seeing beyond their eyes, Joseph in his dreams and Black Bear in his trance visions. This ability gives them power within their tribes, putting them separate from the rest of the people, the people of the village / country, an important power in the coming New Age, the power of seeing beyond the five senses.

For the thirty-five experiences of the group, each experience opened new doors into the Garden, summarized as five new doors as follows.

- The separation experienced in the modern world of learning the knowledge of good and evil has created much dissension, but we overcome this dissension caused by the extreme diversity of life when we learn to appreciate this diversity.

- The residents of the Garden listen to the spirits from beyond the five senses of rationality of the modern world.

- The ancient concept of the Kundalini is alive and well in the new world of the Garden. The strength brought to the individual by repeatedly climbing through the seven chakras to the crown chakra to the birth of light and understanding, and then to return through death to the root chakra, brings them again to a new birth at the crown with greater health and maturity in this cyclic journey to the peak of Goddess-Consciousness.

- Emotions are thought to be a hindrance in the rational discourse of the modern world, but their appreciation adds to the understanding of life in returning to the Garden.

- And, most important in bringing peace to the Garden, the Promised Land, Israel, is wherever the descendants of Abraham dwell.

CHAPTER 12

Trance Experiences that Define Our Lives

The experiences from the seven stories of Genesis were life defining for each person in the group, experiences that carry us to our Goddess-Consciousness. These experiences are summarized here.

Donna

Donna's defining experiences from the beginning take her beyond the Genesis stories and into the new matriarchal world of the Promised Land. Her spirit guide, drawing in the dirt, tells her to not be influenced by the Biblical patriarchal stories, that she knows better. Light enters her heart when punctured with a porcupine quill, bringing her to identify with the matriarchal cycle of conception, birth, life, death, and rebirth that carries her to her Goddess-Consciousness. Her Cain and Abel spirit guides show her the importance of experiencing her connection with nature, as does the Bear of her Noah experience, showing her that everything of the Earth is interconnected.

Journeying with Abraham carries her beyond her crown chakra, bringing alive her spirit body. Following the path of the Matriarchal Cycle of the Kundalini, Donna is carried into the spirit world beyond. Then on her journey with Isaac, she finds herself buried by shamans, the portal to the higher spirituality of her Goddess-Consciousness. With Jacob on the cyclic journey through the Kundalini, when wrapped as a cocoon, she is reborn as part of an intergalactic council. Then finally the Kundalini cycle returns her to the New Garden that is everywhere beyond the geographical Israel, the New Promised Land, where she finds herself in the waters of the Baltic.

Lauren

Lauren's journey through the Genesis stories defines new directions that take her into the matriarchal world of the Promised Land, the New Garden. The wisdom of the Serpent provides her, as it did Eve, with the separating knowledge of good and evil, the patriarchal way of seeking power and control that brings much conflict to the world, causing Cain to kill Abel. But Lauren, as the Queen of the matriarchal underworld, brings these brothers together with her compassion and love. Learning from the drunkenness of Noah, Lauren discovers the selfless responsibility of finding balance between the two worlds, the world of rationality and the world of the spiritual. In journeying with Abraham, she finds she has control over threats on her life by removing her thoughts from the threats. She finds protection in the beautiful shells given to Isaac for protection. Like Jacob, on her journey to return home, she is rescued by a bear, and then by an eagle before a young man of the tribe finds her and provides a place of warmth and food in his teepee with matriarchal love and compassion. Finally, in journeying with Joseph she finds her New Home, The Promised Land, with a tribe in Africa with whom she playfully dances.

Henning

Henning's empathy with the emotions of each experience defines the way he faces life. Emotions, considered an interference to making rational decisions, brings Henning into the New World. In facing the dichotomies of life he learned from the serpent of Eve, he finds truth even in a lie. Henning as Abel, in empathizing with Cain's rat race to impress others, feels resolution with the caresses of the plants of nature. As Noah's dove, he feels fear in entering the unknown world after the flood, but he finds comfort in taking a bath in the dust. Abraham's life is full of pain, first of having to leave the home of his father, and finally in God telling him to sacrifice his son, pain that Henning feels empathetically. The deception experienced by Isaac, with the blessing of Jacob rather than Esau, is discomforting to Henning, but he finds comfort in the honesty of entering his fifth or throat chakra. In journeying with Jacob, the Jacob's ladder dream of the Promised Land extending in all directions to encompass wherever the descendants of Abraham dwell, brings Henning into the New World. He avoids the pain felt in the land of the Canaanites who are in constant battles with invaders. And finally, in Egypt, Henning and Joseph find the matriarchal compassion of the spirits in his new Promised Land. Henning faces with empathy the New World with his Goddess-Consciousness, the New Garden that encompasses the entire Earth.

Lonnie

Lonnie looks to life with positivity. Negative thoughts prevent him from entering the New Garden. In facing the separation of good and evil, with his love for all life when he sees the poisons of commercial agriculture destroying life, he finds comfort in the sun rising each day. He experiences amnesia in facing Cain killing Abel, except for when he is smacked back to awareness. He escapes the destruction of the Earth brought by the Lord to destroy the corruption of the people by flying with all of Earth's life in a rocket ship into space to escape the fires burning on Earth. The people who survive this catastrophe welcome him on his return. Lonnie's Abraham experience is a mountaintop experience where the people come up to him for his blessing. He does not experience the traumatic experiences of Abraham, and he avoids the painful struggle between Jacob and Esau by getting locked out of his house in the dark where he cannot see them fighting. The endless struggle that Jacob had with his Uncle Laban Lonnie sees as an endless circular ride on a carousel where he cannot grab the ring. He then again finds himself on a mountaintop, greeting the people as they come to him for his blessing, and at night he flies above it all as an Eagle. Lonnie finds the new matriarchal Promised Land made green and luscious with his mounted gun that shoots flowers and water. The people are dancing in celebration by the warmth of their fires.

Nick

In facing the conflict that arise in each of the seven stories, I come to them with a new matriarchal perspective. If I eat the fruit from the forbidden tree with the right attitude, an attitude of appreciation, offering gifts in reciprocity to show this appreciation, I can eat it without falling into the world of separation. This reciprocity is also found in honoring the blood of the deer that gave his hide for a drumhead and with the compost to feed the worms and add fertility to the garden. Like Noah's flood, I face crises as opportunities for personal growth. As Abraham, a laughing coyote brought to me by our Great Earth Mother shows me the ridiculousness of sacrificing my son. The voices of the spirits give Isaac direction in life, and hanging on is an effective way to face humiliation for both me and Jacob. And finally on my journey, I find the Promised Land among the Lenni Lenape of Central Pennsylvania. Each experience, when faced with this new perspective, carries me into the new matriarchal world of the New Garden.

The experiences of each of the five of us brought us into the New Garden, defining our lives of personal growth, reaching to our crown chakra with our Goddess-consciousness and our Great Earth Mother in the new way of matriarchy.

CHAPTER 13

Final Words

The Pre-Literate Source of the Stories of Genesis

Before recorded in ancient Hebrew in the Torah, the stories of Genesis or variations of them were passed down orally in other cultures of the time among such people as the Egyptians, Canaanites, and Babylonians. Passed down orally by the bardic shamans of the community, the spirits of these stories were listened to in a deep state of concentration or trance. During the most recent era of rational consciousness, many rationalists have considered these experiences of trance as superstitious or false. But now, as we discover the way back to the Garden, again dreams and trance experiences are accepted and valued.

Our group of five listened to and dwelled on these stories in the state of ecstatic or shamanic trance, a trance induced by the rapid of beat of a drum or a rattle that stimulates our nervous system. The ritual that led us into trance included smudging and calling the spirits from each direction to cleanse and define our space as sacred. We then used five minutes of silence for following to our breath to quiet our minds before entering the 15 minutes of drumming or rattling as we stood, sat, or reclined in an ecstatic posture that gave direction to the trance experience. These postures, as found in ancient art, were believed to have been used by hunting and gathering shamans. At the end of 15 minutes of trance, each person recorded their experience, experiences that became the central content of this book. In this way, we returned to the way of listening as experienced by our ancient hunting and gathering ancestors.

Listening to The Spirits of Each Story

As we listened to the stories of Adam and Eve, Cain and Abel, Noah and the Ark, Abraham, Isaac, Jacob, and Joseph, listening to the spirits of these stories that came to us from beyond our five senses, we found other levels of understanding that opened new doors. Many people in our contemporary world have lost the deeper understanding of these stories because they consider them as literal history. Listening to the spirits in this limited rational manner offers only one dimension to these multidimensional stories.

As described earlier, before the Tower of Babel the ancients heard the first three stories as if the voice of the Lord came from outside of one's body, however after the tower, with the evolutionary development of the two hemispheres of the brain, the ancients heard the voices coming from within, from dreams and visions. Listening to the stories through dreams and visions requires some learning and practice to understand their metaphoric meaning, but when we reached the story of Joseph, we see he excelled in listening to and interpreting dreams, a skill that led him to become the Governor of Egypt, his home as promised him by the Lord. This skill of listening in an altered state of consciousness, in ecstatic trance, is what has taken the five of us in the group to the deeper levels of understanding of the seven stories.

The very ancient concept of the Kundalini, journeying through the seven chakras, is one concept that provided several of the group a deeper avenue to understanding and developing the skill of listening to the spirits. Donna, especially, followed the Kundalini Avenue of seeing beyond her eyes to find fulfillment of the Goddess within her. Though we think of the Kundalini as coming from India, it is much older, found in ancient Egypt, Nubia, and the tribes of Western Africa.

The story of the expulsion of Adam and Eve from the Garden with their gained knowledge of good and evil from eating the forbidden fruit has been very much alive within us for the last several thousand years. The conflicts we experience in life in facing opposing beliefs and opinions have caused much suffering because of the separation these beliefs bring us. Such opposing beliefs, such as what is bad and what is good, what is beautiful and what is ugly, and what is us and what is them come from this knowledge of the dichotomies of good and evil. This knowledge makes us like God, a patriarchal God that uses this knowledge to seek power and control.

The experiences of the five of us have shown that we can overcome this separation by learning to appreciate and value the diversity attributed to these opposing beliefs and opinions. As experienced by Henning, there is truth even in a lie. There is something to learn from this diversity. No one can know everything. We can appreciate and value others who have the knowledge that we lack. Living in this world of great diversity is to be valued for our survival.

Listening to our emotions opens another new gate to the Garden. We have been taught that emotions interfere with making the best decisions, but again, with this teaching, we have lost another important dimension of life in the world of patriarchy. The emotional centers of our brain were early developments in the evolutionary process and valued by our ancient ancestors of the matriarchal world in which they lived. Emotions gave them meaningful direction in life that arose in their trance experiences.

One eye-opener in our experiences came at the end of our journey through the seven stories, that the Garden, the Promised Land, literally considered the land of Israel, is much broader than the land that is now Israel. The Promised Land is wherever we dwell as we find our way back to the Garden. It is not a place, but a frame of mind. Joseph found it in the land of Egypt, Lauren found it in Africa, Donna along the shores of the Baltic Sea, Lonnie found his New Garden in a colder place among trees different from the desert he left, and I found it among the Lenni Lenape people of central Pennsylvania and the Esopus Lenape of the Hudson Valley. We find spiritual growth in each place as it influences our frame of mind. I believe that this discovery in understanding the stories of Genesis can bring peace to the Israeli- Palestinian conflict.

Listening as a Path of Spiritual Growth

Biblically, The Garden of Eden was between the two rivers of Mesopotamia, the Tigris and Euphrates. In our journey to the New Garden, it exists everywhere upon our Earth Mother, and in our Goddess-Consciousness. This New Garden has many names: The New Age, The Age of Aquarius, The Ecstatic Age, The Quantum Age, The Promised Land and The Era of Time-Free Transparency, among them. I feel the last, The Era of Time-Free Transparency, as described by Jean Gebser, nicely describes the way we hear the spirits, free of linear time and transparent in the messages they send to us.

In my previous writings, I have described what I have thought the new Garden will be like. The residents of the new Garden will value the interdependency of all that is of the Earth and support it with the practice of reciprocity. Reciprocity will be a consistent practice of giving back to the Earth as much, if not more than we take. We will live in peace and harmony with all that is of the Earth. Respecting and valuing the diversity of all life will bring about this peace and harmony. We will be part of a close community with those living near us, sharing with one another with love and compassion. In this community, valuing curiosity and continual learning will stimulate creativity within the community and throughout the world.

Our Great Earth Mother will support and provide for the interdependency of all life, sustaining this life in a healthy manner. The experiences of the group support well these traits in the world of time-free transparency. The group also elaborated on the description of life in the Garden in overcoming separation caused by learning the knowledge of good and evil. To overcome the conflicts caused in this world of dichotomies, of opposites, honesty, and the realization that there is truth in a lie are important factors as described in the experiences of Henning. Also, as we look to the world with positive thoughts, peace and harmony will come to the garden as offered in the experiences of Lonnie. Journeying responsibly between the two worlds, the world of the spirits and our physical world, as experienced by Lauren, will bring us the vision for the needed change to save the world from the destruction we, as humans, have imposed upon her. Then, rising to the Goddess that lives within us as experienced by Donna will bring alive the way to live within the Garden, transcending the knowledge of good and evil. Calling upon our compassionate Goddess-Consciousness that exists within each of us, and within all life, rather than the punishing off-planet patriarchal God of separation, opens the gate to the Garden.

The Promised Land

All of us found the Garden to be not just the Promised Land of present-day Israel that has existed in continuous conflict between its inhabitants for several thousand years, including the current Israeli-Palestinian conflict. The Promised Land is wherever we live in a world of compassion and love. Hopefully, we will rise above the current conflicts we see in the world to experience the beauty of peace, harmony, love, and compassion of the matriarchal New Garden.

Notes

Introduction

1. Young, *Snorri Sturluson: The Prose Edda*
2. Graves, *The Greek Myths, Vol. 2*
3. Wright, *Beowulf*
4. Wood, *Seven Herbs: Plants as Teachers*
5. Wood, *Seven Guideposts*
6. Perls, *Gestalt Therapy Verbatim*
7. Brink, *Loki's Children*

Chapter 1: To Begin

1. Brink, *Applying the Constructivist Approach to Cognitive Therapy*, 14-29.
2. Ibid., 34.
3. Ibid., 41-55, 69-103.
4. Ibid., 35.
5. Jaynes, *The Origin of Consciousness in the Break-Down of the Bicameral Mind*.
6. Gebser, *The Ever-Present Origin*.
7. Wood, *Seven Herbs*, 13-14.
8. Ibid., 14.
9. Young, *Snorri Sturluson: The Prose Edda*.
10. Cashford, *The Myth of Isis and Osiris*.
11. Friberg, *The Kalevala*.
12. Elkington, *The Ancient Language of Sacred Sound*.
13. Scranton, *The Science of the Dogon*.

14. Kwesi, *The Origin of the Adam & Eve Story*

15. Graves, *The Greek Myths, Vol. 2.*

16. Wright, *Beowulf.*

17. Calleman, *The Mayan Calendar and the Transformation of Consciousness, 196.*

18. Gebser, *The Ever-Present Origin.*

19. Sheldrake, *The Presence of the Past.*

20. Laszlo, *The Akashic Experience.*

21. Castaneda, *The Eagle's Gift.*

22. Wood, *Seven Guideposts on the Spiritual Path, 7.*

23. Ibid., 11.

Chapter 2: Ecstatic Trance

1. Goodman, *Where the Spirits Ride the Wind.*

2. Emerson, *Can Belief Systems Influence Behavior.*

3. Gore, *Ecstatic Body Postures.*

4. Gore, *The Ecstatic Experience.*

5. Brink, *The Power of Ecstatic Trance.*

6. Brink, *Baldr's Magic.*

7. Brink, *Beowulf's Ecstatic Trance Magic.*

8. Brink, *Trance Journeys of the Hunter-Gatherers.*

9. Brink, *Ecstatic Soul Retrieval.*

10. Brink, *Loki's Children.*

11. Brink, *Applying the Constructivist Approach to Cognitive Therapy.*

12. Brink, *Listening to the Spirits: Surviving the Apocalypse.*

13. Karade, *The Handbook of Yoruba Religious Concepts.*

14. Wood, *Seven Herbs.*

15. Gebser, *The Ever-Present Origin.*

Chapter 3: The Sacred Seven

1. Wood, *Seven Guideposts on the Spiritual Path, 211.*

2. Ibid., 228.

3. Ibid., 241.
4. Ibid., 307.
5. Wood, *Seven Herbs,* 21-40.
6. Ibid., 41-54.
7. Ibid., 55-66.
8. Ibid., 67-84.
9. Ibid., 85-94.
10. Ibid., 95-108.
11. Ibid., 109-120.
12. Bynum.
13. Scranton.
14. Karade.
15. Blue Eagle.
16. Karade., 47-54.
17. Bynum.
18. Blue Eagle.
19. Kenyon & Sion, 94, 120-124.
20. Ibid., 190.
21. Gebser.
22. Scheffer, *Lapponia,* 139.

Chapter 4: Adam anad Eve

1. Bertrand & Bertrand, *Womb Awakening,* 172-180.

Chapter 5: Cain and Abel

1. Wood, *Seven Herbs,* 47.
2. Harner, *The Way of the Shaman.*
3. Gebser.

Chapter 9: Isaac

1. Ralston.

Chapter 11: Returning to the Garden

1.   Gebser.
2.   Genesis 28:13-14.

Bibliography

Bertrand, Azra & Bertrand, Seren. *Womb Awakening: Initiatory Wisdom from the Creatrix of All Life.* Rochester, VT: Bear & Company, 2017.

Bertrand, Seren. *Spirit Weaver: Wisdom Teachings from the Feminine Path of Magic.* Rochester, VT: Bear & Company, 2022.

Blue Eagle, Luke. *First Nation Crystal Healing: Working with Teachers of the Mineral Kingdom.* Rochester, VT: Bear & Company, 2021.

Brink, Nicholas. *Grendel and His Mother: Healing the Traumas of Childhood Through Dreams, Imagery and Hypnosis.* New York, NY: Routledge, 2019.

_____, *The Power of Ecstatic Trance: Practices for Healing, Spiritual Growth, and Accessing the Universal Mind.* Rochester, VT: Bear & Company, 2013.

_____, *Baldr's Magic: The Power of Norse Shamanism and Ecstatic Trance.* Rochester, VT: Bear & Company. 2014.

_____, *Beowulf's Ecstatic Trance Magic: Accessing the Archaic Powers of the Universal Mind.* Rochester, VT: Bear & Company, 2016.

_____, *Trance Journeys of the Hunter-Gatherers: Ecstatic Practices to Reconnect with the Great Mother and Heal the Earth.* Rochester, VT: Bear & Company, 2016.

_____, *Ecstatic Soul Retrieval: Shamanism and Psychotherapy.* Rochester, VT: Bear & Company, 2017.

_____, *Applying The Constructivist Approach to Cognitive Therapy: Resolving the Unconscious Past,* New York, NY: Routledge, 2019.

_____, *Loki's Children: A Healing Story of Antiquity, Shamanism and Psychotherapy.* Rhinebeck, NY: Red Elixir, 2022.

_____, *Listening to the Spirits: Surviving the Coming Apocalypse with Ecstatic Trance*. Rhinebeck, NY: Red Elixir, 2022.

Bynum, Edward. *Our African Unconscious: The Black Origins of Mysticism and Psychology,* Rochester, VT: Inner Traditions, 2021.

Calleman, Carl. *The Mayan Calendar and the Transformation of Consciousness*. Rochester, VT: Bear & Company, 2004.

Cashford, Jules. *The Myth of Isis and Osiris*. Boston, MA: Barefoot Books, 1993.

Castaneda, Carlos. *The Eagle's Gift*. New York, NY: Washington Square Press, 1991.

Elkington, David, *The Ancient Language of Sacred Sound: The Acoustic Science of the Divine*. Rochester, VT: Inner Traditions, 2021.

Emerson, V. F. "Can Belief Systems Influence Behavior? Some Implications of Research on Meditation," *Newsletter Review*. R. M. Bucke Memorial Society, 5:20-32.

Friberg, Eino (translator). *The Kalevala: Epic of the Finnish People*. Helsinki, Finland: Otava Publishing Co., 1988.

Gebser, Jean. *The Ever-Present Origin*. Athens, OH: Ohio University Press, 1982.

Goodman, Felicitas. *Where the Spirits Ride the Wind: Trance Journeys and Other Ecstatic Experiences*. Bloomington, IA: Indiana University Press, 1990.

Gore, Belinda. *Ecstatic Body Postures: An Alternate Reality Workbook*. Rochester, VT: Bear & Company, 1995.

_____, *The Ecstatic Experience: Healing Postures for Spirit Journeys*. Rochester, VT: Bear & Company, 2009.

Graves, Robert. *The Greek Myths, Vol. 2*. New York, NY: Penguin Books, 1960.

Harner, Michael. *The Way of the Shaman*. San Francisco, CA: Harper One, 1990.

Holy Bible: The King James Version, New York, NY: The World Publishing Company.

Jaynes, Julian. *The Origin of Consciousness in the Break-Down of the Bicameral Mind*. Boston, MA: Houghton Mifflin Company, 1976.

Karade, Baba Ifa. *The Handbook of Yoruba Religious Concepts.* Newburyport, MA: Red Wheel / Weiser, 2020.

Kenyon, Tom & Judi Sion. *The Magdalen Manuscript: The Alchemies of Horus & The Sex Magic of Isis,* Orcas, WA: ORB Communications, 2002.

Kwesi, Ashra. *The Origin of the Adam & Eve Story,* YouTube, Kemetnu6240, 2009.

Laszlo, Ervin. *The Akashic Experience: Science and the Cosmic Memory Field.* Rochester, VT: Inner Traditions, 2009.

Perls, Frederick. *Gestalt Therapy Verbatim.* Gouldsboro, ME: Gestalt Journal Press, 1992.

Ralston, Peter. *The Book of Not Knowing: Exploring the True Nature of Self, Mind and Consciousness,* Berkeley, CA: North Atlantic Books, 2010.

Robinson, James, Editor, *The Nag Hammadi Library,* New York, NY: HarperCollins, 1990.

Scheffer, S. J., *Lapponia,* Frankfurt, Germany, 1673.

Scranton, Laird. *The Science of the Dogon: Decoding the African Mystery Tradition.* Rochester, VT: Inner Traditions, 2006.

Sheldrake, Rupert. *The Presence of the Past: Morphic Resonance and the Habits of Nature.* Rochester, VT: Park Street Press,1995.

Wood, Matthew. *Seven Herbs: Plants as Teachers.* Berkeley, CA: North Atlantic Books, 1987.

_____, *Seven Guideposts on the Spiritual Path: The Shamanic Stories of Genesis.* Spring Valley, WI: Matthew Wood Institute of Herbalism, 2021.

Wright, David (translator). *Beowulf.* New York, NY: Penguin Books, 1957.

Young, Jean (translator). *Snorri Sturluson: The Prose Edda: Tales from Norse Mythology.* Berkeley, CA: University of California Press, 1954.

www.ingramcontent.com/pod-product-compliance
Lightning Source LLC
Chambersburg PA
CBHW022131080426
42734CB00006B/312